Jack Allanach has been writing professionally for many years – for television and magazines, and for corporate clients, primarily in the information technology and telecommunications industries. *Colour Me Healing* is his first book, and is also published in German. He and his wife live in Sydney, Australia.

Peter Mandel, creator of Colourpuncture

Colour Me Healing

Colourpuncture: A New Medicine of Light

Jack Allanach

vega

First published by Element Books Ltd 1997

ISBN 1-84333-124-1

A catalogue record for this book is available from the British Library

Published in 2002 by
Vega
64 Brewery Road
London, N7 9NT

A member of Chrysalis Books plc

Visit our website at www.chrysalisbooks.co.uk

Printed in Great Britain
by Lightning Source
Cover designed by Design Revolution, Brighton

To
Peter Mandel
for being who he is

Contents

List of Figures

Acknowledgements

For such a seemingly solo process as writing a book, there are a great many other people involved. For their generous help and inspiration I should like to express particular gratitude to Peter Mandel, for his constant availability, cooperation and trust; Verena Allanach, my loving wife, for so beautifully bridging the language barrier between Mandel and me, and for the clarity of her insight and her keen Virgo eye; Dr Jaldhara Kristen, for her inexhaustible patience in guiding me, particularly in the early days, through unfamiliar medical territory; Dr Fausto Pagnamenta, Markus Wunderlich, Martina Schupeta, Franz Kohl, Robert Füss, Rosemary Dass, Eduardo Zaba, Manohar Croke, Lyn White, John Barlow, Angelika Hochadel and all the other doctors, naturopaths and Colourpuncturists who shared their experience and case histories with me; Margot Graf, Martina Mandel, Rosita Mandel, Birgit Henneges and Andreas Pflegler for their welcome and assistance on our visits to Bruchsal; Dr Fritz-Albert Popp, for his Introduction and for sharing the results of his pioneering research into the mysteries of light and cellular communication; Sarita and Danish Lena, for first introducing me, via the Transmitter Relays, to Colourpuncture; Dieter Hagenbach, my agent, for his confidence in the project from the beginning; Michael Mann, Chairman and Publisher of Element Books, for agreeing that it was important this story be told; editor John Baldock for suggesting how to fine-tune the telling; and my editor Florence Hamilton for so beautifully seeing the book through to publication; and Osho, for setting me on the path to myself.

Copyright acknowledgements

Grateful acknowledgement is made for permission to reprint the following.

Excerpt from *The Awakening Earth* by Peter Russell, copyright 1991 by Peter Russell. Reprinted by permission of Penguin Books Ltd.

Excerpt from *Blackfoot Physics* by F David Peat, copyright 1994 by F David Peat. Reprinted by permission of Fourth Estate Ltd.

Excerpt from *The Fountainhead* by Ayn Rand published by HarperCollins, granted by permission of Laurence Pollinger Ltd and Simon & Schuster US. © 1943 by the Bobbs–Merrill Company Inc. Copyright renewed 1970 by Ayn Rand.

Excerpt from *The Holographic Universe* by Michael Talbot, copyright 1991 by Michael Talbot. Reprinted by permission of HarperCollins Publishers Ltd.

Excerpt from *Heal Your Body* by Louise L Hay, copyright 1988 by Louise L Hay. Reprinted by permission of Specialist Publications.

Excerpt from *Light: Medicine of the Future* by Jacob Liberman, copyright 1991 by Jacob Liberman, OD, PhD. Reprinted by permission of Bear & Co., Santa Fe, NM, USA.

Excerpt from *Love, Medicine & Miracles* by Bernie S Siegel MD, copyright 1986 by B H Siegel, S Korman and A Schiff, Trustees of the Bernard S Siegel MD Children's Trust. Reprinted by permission of Peters Fraser & Dunlop Ltd.

Excerpt from *The Man Who Mistook His Wife for a Hat* by Oliver Sacks, copyright 1985 by Oliver Sacks. Reprinted by permission of Gerald Duckworth & Co Ltd.

Excerpt from *Quantum Healing* by Deepak Chopra MD, copyright 1989 by Deepak Chopra. Reprinted by permission of Bantam Books.

Excerpt from *The Secret of the Atomic Age* by Vera Stanley Alder, copyright 1988, Estate of Vera Stanley Alder. Reprinted by permission of Rider Books.

Excerpt from *The Tibetan Book of Living and Dying* by Sogyal Rinpoche, copyright 1993 by Ripga Fellowship. Reprinted by permission of HarperCollins Publishers Ltd.

Excerpt from *Vibrational Medicine* by Dr Richard Gerber, copyright 1988 by Dr Richard Gerber. Reprinted by permission of Bear & Co., Santa Fe, NM, USA.

The reproductions of the Kirlian photographs of the two patients are reprinted by permission of Dr J Kristen.

All other material pertaining to Peter Mandel, including illustrations, photographs and excerpts from any of his books is reprinted by permission of Energetik Versand und Verlags GmbH, Bruchsal, Germany.

With regard to *The Intelligent Universe* by David Foster, published in 1975, despite various attempts it has been hitherto impossible to trace the owner of the rights to this title. However, should the copyright holder make him- or herself known, the author will be happy to make full acknowledgement in any subsequent reprint.

Foreword

We know today that man, essentially, is a being of light. And the modern science of photobiology, as you will discover in these pages, is presently proving this. In terms of healing (the subject of this book) the implications are immense. We now know, for example, that quanta of light can initiate, or arrest, cascade-like reactions in the cells, and that genetic cellular damage can be virtually repaired, within hours, by faint beams of light. We are still on the threshold of fully understanding the complex relationship between light and life, but we can now say, emphatically, that the function of our entire metabolism is dependent on light.

Colour Me Healing is the story of the founding and evolution of a new medicine of light by the outstanding German scientist and healer, Peter Mandel. Through conversations with Mandel, his own experience of Colourpuncture (Mandel's therapeutic methodology of light) and anecdotes from both their lives, Jack Allanach has bridged the worlds of healer and patient, of scientist and layman, to open a new window on the disharmony we call 'sickness' and the harmony we call 'health'.

I first came to know and appreciate Peter Mandel some ten years ago, as the pioneer of a new technique for medical diagnosis based on Kirlian photography. He recognized very quickly the unforeseen possibilities this method offers to medicine. And it is the mark of a true pioneer that this discovery soon led him to others – and one of the most significant is that we are light-beings who can respond to treatment with colours, the components of light.

Peter Mandel is distinguished by an explosive mixture of imagination and realism. This is clearly revealed by his tireless investigation into the mysteries of therapy, by the development of models for understanding the organization of living structures and, last but not least, by his compassion for others and his strong commitment to helping those who are ill. The harmony Peter Mandel seeks in all things, he instils in those who put themselves into his care. I see these as the fundamental factors in his undeniable success.

During my studies we had a teacher who, witnessing our often lamentable efforts to dive deeper into the mysteries of quantum physics, remarked repeatedly that the mark of a good physicist would be – if the physicist were a doctor – that he would be able to entrust his children to this physicist.

I often remember this incident from my student years when I think of Peter Mandel. Not only does he possess the essential requirements of a scientist – a sense of responsibility coupled with the ability to travel new and unknown paths – he is *the* healer to whom I would entrust my own children.

Dr Fritz-Albert Popp
Visiting Professor (mult) of Biophysics
Managing Director
Technology Centre
International Institute of Biophysics
Kaiserslautern

Preface

There are some things in life that just have to be shared. Like kisses or recipes, fine wine or good news. And that's why *Colour Me Healing* came to be. Peter Mandel's Colourpuncture was too remarkable to be kept to myself, or limited to my small circle of friends.

Colourpuncture is a new medicine, with all the ramifications for diagnosis and treatment the word implies. And what sets Colourpuncture apart from its predecessors – from homoeopathy and allopathy, naturopathy and acupuncture – is that it contains a new key to prevention as well. After 30 years of clinical observation and experimentation, Mandel has identified where physical illness begins. And he's discovered how to halt its destructive course. To me, this is news to be shouted from the rooftops.

So is what Mandel can do for those who are already sick. As Colourpuncture is not yet mainstream it's often a last resort, and his clinic is swamped, for example, with cancer sufferers orthodox medicine has given up for dead. Within a quarter of a year of treatment, some forty per cent of these so-called 'terminal' patients are either free of cancer or free of debilitating symptoms, gaining weight and enjoying a whole new lease of life despite this severe disease. Given the advanced condition the great majority of these people arrive in, Mandel's success rate is impressive indeed.

As we approach the next millennium, it's painfully obvious that the limits of traditional medicine have been reached. It's time for a new dispensation, for seeking the secret to health inside ourselves, not outside in some pharmaceutical lab. It's time to harness the healing power of the life-force itself, the energy of light. In *Light: Medicine of the Future*, Dr Jacob Liberman calls it 'healing ourselves with that which is our essence'. And this is precisely what Peter Mandel is doing. Colourpuncture heralds the dawning of a new era in medicine, the aeon of light.

I'm neither a medical practitioner nor a scientist; *Colour Me Healing* has been written for ordinary men and women, for people like me. It embodies, however, another hope – that it will also speak to healing professionals, that it will trigger, in them, an urge to explore the healing art of Peter Mandel. For, in truth, he is a light for our time, a giant among men.

Jack Allanach
Sydney, Australia

1

A light in the darkness

Only the best art can order the chaotic tumble of events.
MICHAEL ONDAATJE
In the Skin of a Lion

They come from everywhere – from neighbouring towns; from distant cities and far-off lands. And most of them come because they've been everywhere else. They've visited all the specialists; they've tried all the cures. They come because they've heard reports of this Peter Mandel, of this man who works wonders with rays of coloured light.

One afternoon in 1990 yet another sufferer arrived in the German town of Bruchsal, hoping against hope. And at the corner opposite the railway station, he found the address he'd been given. Albert, as we'll call him, was in his late sixties, but he took the stairs to the second-floor clinic like someone half his age. He wasn't here for himself; he was here for his wife, for Hilda – and he felt in his heart there wasn't a moment to lose.

'I must see Mr Mandel urgently,' he insisted to the receptionist the second he burst through the door. He was so obviously distraught, so close to total panic, that she arranged for Mandel to squeeze him in between appointments, to see him almost right away.

'My wife is dying of cancer!' he announced desperately. 'She's in hospital in a coma and the doctors say there's nothing they can do!' On Mandel's desk Albert laid a computer tomogram of Hilda's brain showing it riddled with metastases, revealing just how far the malignancy had spread. 'I know it's bad,' he said sombrely, 'but please tell me there is *something* you can do!'

Did he have a copy of her medical history? Albert handed it over. It painted a picture of a life of pain and suffering, a life spent in and out of sickbeds and hospitals since 1942, when Hilda was only 18.

That year, she contracted diphtheria, and three years later, hepatitis. Then, at 28, came the first of many encounters with the surgeon's knife. A tumour was removed from an ovary, and there was a gall-bladder operation as well.

At 32, she was diagnosed with bone tuberculosis – a prelude to a succession of bone, joint and spinal ailments that was to begin in earnest when she was 51 and plague her for the next 15 years.

Before the real onset of this rheumatic deterioration, however, there were still other difficulties to face. When Hilda was 34, she delivered a child prematurely, by Caesarean section, and six years afterwards, had her uterus and ovaries removed. In the period after this operation, she also began to suffer from chronic haemorrhoidal pain.

By age 53, Hilda was virtually crippled – disabled by osteoporosis and incapacitated by severe bone and joint pain all over her body. Then, at 60, she was diagnosed with Bechterew's disease, *ankylosing spondylitis*, that chronic, rheumatic inflammation that attacks the aged in particular, robbing them of mobility, stiffening their spines and, in the most extreme cases, bending them almost double.

In 1989, when she was 65, she returned to the hospital for an operation to relieve the distress of her haemorrhoids. But while preparing her for surgery, the doctors discovered cancer. And they removed her right lung. A year later she found herself back in intensive care, this time with metastases in the brain.

'Now she's in a coma and they tell me she's going to die,' Albert said to Mandel. 'Over the years, I've taken her everywhere, followed every suggestion, tried every avenue. If you say you can't help me either, then there's nowhere left to go!'

Mandel had no intention of turning Albert away. Like best-selling American physician-authors Bernie Siegel and Deepak Chopra, he has developed his own method for combating cancer. His focus: eliminate the root cause that's triggered the cancer in the first place.

That cause, Mandel states, is unresolved emotional conflict. And in this assertion he is not alone. Siegel and Chopra fundamentally say the same thing. But where one counsels love and the other recommends meditation, Mandel uses Colourpuncture to shine a light on the conflict, to bring it to conscious awareness where it can be encountered, dealt with and resolved.

Colourpuncture uses light and its component colours to reintroduce the correct 'informative energy' into the mind/body complex wherever wrong 'information' has become lodged – through traumas like childhood abuse, unshed tears, thwarted self-expression, repressed anger, relationship breakdown, or any of the myriad influences that contribute to misshaping our lives. It's rather like eradicating viruses in our biocomputer's software.

In Colourpuncture, the colour is the message, and the medium is coloured light – focused on specific point combinations on the skin via coloured rods of quartz glass inserted into a stainless-steel, battery-operated torch about the size of a Havana cigar.

Mandel provided Albert with a Colourpuncture set, and taught him how to administer the 'Conflict Solving' therapy, his system for treating the unresolved emotional conflicts that he sees as the root cause of cancer and other degenerative diseases. He told Albert to perform the treatment on Hilda twice a day, and to keep him informed. Within ten days Hilda awoke from the coma and, in another ten, was able to leave the hospital.

As soon as she was sufficiently fit, Albert brought her to the clinic for more intensive treatment with Conflict Solving and other Colourpuncture systems. Then, nine weeks after her discharge from hospital, Mandel decided it was time to take another look at what was happening in Hilda's brain. The new computer tomogram showed no trace of cancer whatsoever.

At the hospital, this created an uproar! Faced with the inexplicable, the doctors didn't know what to say – so they insisted there must have been a switch, that the original tomogram must have belonged to someone else, that Hilda couldn't really have had cancer after all.

And why this duplicity? Because allopathic doctors stick together; because results like this expose the limitations of Western medicine; and because to acknowledge Mandel's success in treating cancer – especially with a system designed to address such an unorthodox cause as unresolved emotional conflict – means to admit that allopathy is not only focused on symptoms rather than origins, but is also based on a fundamental misunderstanding of how the mind/body complex, in its totality, actually works.

In the past, Mandel allowed, this blind prejudice on the part of the medical establishment used to hurt. 'But not any more,' he shrugged as he related this story. 'I don't have to prove to science that I'm right. They have to prove to me that I'm wrong.'

That's not going to be easy. Patients like Hilda and Albert swear by him; his colleagues rank him among naturopathy's greats. And his foundations are solid. His medicine of light is grounded in humanity's most ancient wisdom and in the findings of modern biophysics. He calls it 'Esogetic' medicine: *eso* from esoteric; *getic* from energetic. And it incorporates an understanding of the human being as new as it is old.

For instance: down the ages mystics have maintained that our physical body is the grossest expression of a far greater phenomenon, and that an energy body, or aura, surrounds the physical body like a sleeve. Peter Mandel says it is here, in this energy body, that illness really begins. And the cause is conflict. If left unresolved, if left to fester, conflicts will eventually manifest as matter, solidifying into tangible sickness on the material plane. A physical symptom is simply the final link in a very long chain.

Although we may not remember intellectually, it is Mandel's view that the conflicts of adulthood are always repetitions of those which began in childhood or in the prenatal time.

During the time he treated Hilda in the Bruchsal clinic, these were the periods of her life on which he focused, with special treatments and systems we'll explore in chapters to come. And whatever Hilda's conflict – Mandel didn't volunteer the information and I didn't feel it right to pry – she spent her next years free of cancer and free of pain.

To be with family, Hilda and Albert had left Germany for Canada in the early 1990s. And from there, in 1995, Albert wrote to say that Hilda, then 71, had died – after new and inoperable tumours suddenly appeared in her remaining lung.

'He told me that the five years before her death were without pain,' Mandel said, 'and this was for the very first time in her adult life!

'He said she died easily, and that she was serene and quite radiant when they said their final goodbye.

'And he thanked me – on behalf of both of them – for the quality of her last five years.'

The language of the cells

Mandel's successes prove that light and colour applied to the skin – the line of demarcation between the physical and energy bodies – can trigger a harmonizing, and therefore a healing impulse in both spheres. He claims Colourpuncture can neutralize conflicts before they develop into disease, eradicate illnesses that have already taken hold, and in the case of patients with histories like Hilda's, give them a new and pain-free lease of life.

One of the secrets lies in the physics of cellular communication. Dr Fritz-Albert Popp, 'the father of the biophoton theory', discovered that normal living cells emit a regular stream of photons, or quanta of light radiation – and in his book *Biologie des Lichts* (Biology of Light) he documents evidence to prove that living cells pass on biological information through photons, through the language of light.

One of the first to point towards light as the language of cellular communication was the Russian biologist Alexander G Gurwitsch, back in 1922. Just as the flame of a candle is able to jump from a lighted candle to ignite the wick of an unlit one, Gurwitsch observed that the cells of an onion stalk began the process of mitosis, the division into new cells, as soon as they were approached by the roots of another onion.

At the time, the popular theory was that the regulation of cell growth was the responsibility of chemical messenger molecules – but Gurwitsch was convinced the 'messenger' was actually light, in the form of a low-level luminescence he'd detected in living tissues.[1] To demonstrate his hypothesis, and avoid any possibility of the onions physically touching, Gurwitsch separated them by glass. With ordinary window glass, nothing happened, but with quartz glass, which allows ultraviolet radiation to pass through it, the process of cell division in the second onion was stimulated. In other words, the message of growth was transmitted.

In his book, Dr Popp reports on the work of three other Soviet scientists – S Stschurin, V P Kaznacheev and L Michailova – who showed in more than 5,000 experiments conducted 50 years later that light is, indeed, the carrier of biological information.

In one definitive experiment, living cells in a nutrient solution were placed in two hermetically sealed quartz-glass containers with the side of one jar just touching the side of the other. The cells in one container were infected with a virus and, almost simultaneously, the cells in the neighbouring vessel became sick as well. The fascinating thing is that the virus itself was not transmitted: the infected cells simply broadcast the information that they were ill.

These experiments point to two conclusions: one, cells communicate bio-information; and two, they do so via the medium of light.

And what is light? Light is a combination of the colours of the rainbow, of the spectrum from red to violet – and mankind has known for thousands of years that each colour bears a specific relationship to our health and well-being.

This, in essence, is the basis of Colourpuncture. It beams straight to afflicted cells with the harmonizing information inherent in colour – and the healing news is shouted from cell to cell.

In developing an actual Colourpuncture therapy, the catalyst that sparks a system can come, according to Mandel, from virtually anywhere. From a dream, a hunch, a holographic flash; from a remark he's overheard, a television programme he's seen, a book he's read.

Intuition also plays an important part. And yes, he admits, there *is* another source, but it's one he can't explain. Many of his treatments come to him in sudden 'flashes'. They are suddenly just 'there', available, sometimes as fragments, sometimes as complete systems, but he has no idea from whence they come. After years of wondering, Mandel has finally stopped asking. All he knows or cares about today is that his systems work.

Rewriting the script

For an example of how a Colourpuncture system develops, let's look at one called 'Transmitter Relays'. It's a system Mandel used in treating Hilda after her coma, and it is also the system that first introduced Colourpuncture to me.

In a phrase, the purpose of the Transmitter Relays therapy is to clear old traumas and pave the way for one's individual potential, one's own unique 'life program', to manifest unimpeded.

Mandel said it was while reading about the chakras[2] in Indian esoteric literature that he began thinking in the direction that led to the discovery of the Transmitter Relays.

As he read, he began viewing the chakras as centres of informative energy – 'that which turns dead matter into living matter', to quote German psychologist Frederic Vester – and, indeed, as the very organizational model of life itself.

'In my opinion, information is not only part of everything that lives, but it is also individually designed for each living being,' Mandel wrote in his first, self-published book, *Esogetics: The Sense and Nonsense of Sickness and Pain.* And if a person repeatedly contravenes his own program, this will lead 'to a blockage of the overriding information, and trigger, in turn, disorders in a great number of subordinate functions'. And the result? The person gets sick.

It's generally agreed that the cosmos feeds us with informative energy through the seven chakras or 'intake valves' located in the aura, and that this cosmic energy is then metabolized and directed to the nearest major nerve plexus for subsequent distribution.

Mandel, however, suspected that metabolizing cosmic energy wasn't quite that simple. He'd pored over accounts of ancient Egyptian initiation rites, reports of the methodical preparation of acolytes to receive this cosmic energy in its purity. Too much, too fast, they said, and our circuits would blow. There must be an inbuilt filtering system, Mandel surmised, that allows us to assimilate the precise informative energies required to fulfil our individual purpose here.

From a combination of intuition and dreams, clinical observation and his own intuitive intelligence, he finally located where this filtering happens: in seven circular 'switching stations' on the skin, distributed over the body. He named them the Transmitter Relays.

One relay, he discovered, governs the immune system; a second, our drives, like survival and sex; and four others deal with 'the spirit within the cells'.

The final relay, on the forehead, he dubbed the Relay of Memories. Here, he said, 'every change, every instant of our lives is recorded'. And also here is the life program, the incarnational blueprint, inscribed at the moment of conception – with the information it carries activated by birth.

In computing parlance, there's a practice called 'data compression' – a method of compacting information for more efficient transmission. And this, it would seem, is what existence does as well. It's as if one's entire horoscope were condensed into a microdot and imprinted on the forehead – ready to de-compress, to unfold, as we live out our lives.

Assuming existence is innately beneficent – as I have come to do – then what goes wrong? Why are we regularly out of sorts, frustrated and unfulfilled? And why are we so often ill?

Much of the time it's because of unresolved traumas, which, like experience, teach us the lessons we are here to learn. It's how life ripens us; it's how we evolve. But some shocks can be so totally annihilating that shoving them down into the subconscious is, at the moment, the only way to survive. Or they can be karmic, unremembered, rooted in another incarnation. Either way, left incomplete, they can cause us to be maladjusted emotionally or can make us physically sick. It is in freeing these deep, unconscious traumas that Colourpuncture, and the Transmitter Relays in particular, excel.

'Fallen logs can change the course of a river,' Mandel said. 'In the same way traumas create blocks that divert the energy from its natural flow, forcing us into the same groove over and over, into repeating the same patterns again and again.' In the hands of a good therapist, Colourpuncture can spotlight these blocks. And the client's willingness and awareness can shift them out of the way.

Which is precisely what happened for me.

In a man's search for a life partner psychologists say that he is basically seeking a photocopy of his mother – and when a boy's been told that his mother died of birth complications, a legacy of guilt and low self-worth is bound to pervert this pursuit. And so, when it came to attracting women, I always got precisely what I believed I deserved.

A couple of years back, after aeons in an emotional desert, everything changed: I underwent a series of ten sessions of Colourpuncture that finally ushered love into my life. This was no selfless love for mankind, no saintly adoration of the divine, but the heart-to-heart, spirit-to-spirit, flesh-to-flesh love of a man for a woman and a woman for a man, extraordinary in its ordinariness.

And do I credit these ten Colourpuncture sessions with this? Yes and no. I credit them with bringing to conscious awareness the hidden agenda that had alienated me, keeping me alone for so many years. I credit myself with the intelligence to have seen the pattern and let it go – and when Verena stood before me, I credit myself with the courage to have recognized her and to have accepted life's gift of love.

A friend involved me in the particular Transmitter Relays series that transformed my life. A seminar to teach the technique to a group of 15 therapists from eight countries was being organized, and for purposes of demonstration they wanted a model to articulate what was happening at each stage. Knowing my mouth, my friend came to me.

The whole idea of coloured lights and 'informative energies' sounded preposterous until I actually sat down and had a long think about it, about the life-giving light of the sun and about information, like the individual data we carry in our DNA.[3] Why not? I concluded.

I decided to give it a go.

There were a couple of reasons.

First, some things needed looking at. My mother died when I was two months old and my first stepmother died when I was five – and these deaths had established a pattern that drew me to women destined to leave. But the root cause, the actual incident that had initiated this abandonment syndrome, I'd never been able to locate and resolve. It was buried away somewhere, locked in the forgetfulness of those early, formative years. Colourpuncture could well be the ticket. Something to shine a light in the darkness. Literally.

Second, the day I was asked to participate was my birthday.

So I said yes.

I showed up for the first session to find myself positioned on a pallet in the centre of a group of 15 strangers. But after the first hour I began to relax. Eyes closed, gaze turned in on myself, everyone disappeared; to all intents and purposes there was no one in the room but the therapist and me.

From the first session through to the tenth, my mind swung between impotence and even greater impotence. Colourpuncture gave it nothing to cling to, nothing to compute. Whatever experience I'd had to date, therapeutic or otherwise, there'd always been something to which my mind could relate – some association or context, some point of reference – but here there was nothing. Playfully, painlessly and non-intrusively, coloured lights were being shone on my forehead and miracles were happening inside. And with my analytical faculties relegated to uselessness, all I could do was watch. All I could do was *see*.

The colours used in a specific Colourpuncture treatment are clearly prescribed; whereas the points on the skin where the light is to be applied can only be indicated approximately, usually within a millimetre or two. For treatment, points must be located precisely, and this is done by testing with a blunt, pencil-like tool. Sensitivity is the gauge. When pressure on a point is painful, something is amiss in the energy flow.

One session revealed such an imbalance – a deep one from the intensity of my reaction – during my months in the womb.

Shocks that occur during this time are especially difficult to neutralize, Mandel said. 'This is because they have nothing to do with intellect. During the majority of the time in the womb the intellectual part of the brain, the neo-cortex, has not been finished.

But the midbrain has. And it is here that emotional shocks register, creating blocks in the limbic system.'

The limbic system is the fundamental connection between body and emotion. It houses emotional responses like joy and anger, thirst and hunger, tension and relaxation. It's also the repository of emotional memory.

'If there's a prenatal shock to the limbic system, it will set a pattern in motion that can plague a man throughout his whole life,' Mandel explained. 'And it will be almost impossible to free himself from this pattern, even if he is aware of it intellectually. On an emotional level, the prenatal period determines how a person is going to create his life, or destroy it.'

The latent influence of this time in the womb was identified by England's Robert St John during the evolution of his widely practised prenatal massage in the mid-1950s. There is, St John concluded, a stage of 'preconception choices', a phase Mandel calls 'the knitting of the plan.'

Modern psychology acknowledges that the root of many traumas can be traced to the womb. A feeling of not being wanted, for example, can often be linked to a mother's having considered abortion during pregnancy.

Colourpuncture's Prenatal therapy – which Mandel developed from St John's prenatal massage and then expanded considerably – is conducted on the feet, with point sensitivity indicating when a shock occurred. In my case, when the therapist probed one particular spot it felt like a steel spike had been driven into my instep. 'This would be at around six months,' she said.

When the light was applied my womb-world collapsed. My environment was suddenly threatened; my very survival in jeopardy. It was like I was being sucked into the eye of a cyclone or swept out to sea. My mother had reached a conscious decision to die!

I vacated my body in that same split second, catapulting to another level of consciousness. And hovering there, between dimensions, I realized that this death that I'd taken personally, and carried as a lifelong burden, had had nothing to do with me. Her reason was private, rooted in a conflict with my father she was helpless to resolve. Fifty years ago, in a little town in Canada, a married woman was still a chattel, and she took the only exit she could see.

It's said that our souls choose the circumstances of each incarnation, and I also saw why I'd selected this womb. It was precisely because, in this life, the mother wasn't going to be around. I needed her absence to contact my own inner woman, to connect to the softness and receptivity that is an integral, yet ordinarily denied component of the total man. This mother was simply a vehicle, a passage. She grew my body in hers and gave it birth. And we went our separate ways.

Then, as abruptly as I'd left my body, I was back again. And I opened my eyes to a script rewritten. I felt no more confusion, no more guilt. Just cleansed and worthy and wonderfully free.

The Transmitter Relays met my friend's promise. Pattern seen; pattern neutralized. And a new door opened. Wherever my life program wanted to lead, I was ready to follow.

Underlying everything was an unexpected yet undeniable knowing: that I would write about this Peter Mandel; that his healing systems *had* to be shared! What I didn't know yet was that the delicate Swiss lady in the training, the one with the earnest green eyes and the white Indira Gandhi streak in her long brown hair, was to become my lover, my best friend and, a year later, my wife.

Meeting the medicine man

Our first encounter with Peter Mandel took place in a luxury hotel in Switzerland, overlooking the lake at Lucerne. We waited in the lounge for a break in a seminar he was conducting for doctors, naturopaths and therapists from German-speaking Europe. When the doors opened and the participants spilled out, heading for the coffee urns, we spotted Peter Mandel immediately. Charisma is hard to miss.

At first he was surprised and bemused when Verena told him I wanted to write a book about him. But when she translated my enthusiasm for his Transmitter Relays therapy, he broke into a sudden grin. 'OK,' he nodded, 'why not?' That, I discovered, was pretty much it for his English.

I was also aware that I'd been checked out thoroughly.

I didn't mind, because the second I'd shaken his hand I knew my gut feeling had been right. This, in the Gurdjieffian[4] sense, was a meeting with a remarkable man. I didn't understand his words, but as he talked to Verena I tasted their timbre, their tone. I liked what I heard, and when I looked into his eyes I liked who I saw.

His eyes shone with clarity, humour and intelligence. He was open and unassuming, and reassuringly ordinary: as we talked he smoked with enjoyment and downed a chilled beer with gusto. There is a vitality about him that belies his 56 years.

During the Transmitter Relays I'd been told he 'channelled' his Colourpuncture systems. I said so to him. Not in the 'American sense', he chuckled. If there's some spirit broadcasting to him from another world, some Emmanuel or Seth,[5] he's never identified himself.

We all agreed 'conduit' was a better word.

Whether the source is external or internal, cosmic flash or inner hunch; whether the inspiration comes as a fragment or a total system, it still has to be developed into a practical therapy he can use on his patients. But first he always experiments on himself; only then does he apply it to others to observe their reactions, to assess their responses. 'My practice is my laboratory,' he said. It's where he's been honing his skills for the last 30 years.

The pillars of Mandel's Esogetic medicine may be mankind's most ancient wisdom and the light research of modern biophysics, but the architect of the edifice is the man himself. The genius, the inquisitiveness are his. And so are the cosmic flashes.

He's deciphered a healing code on the human skin. He's researched which combination of acupuncture points can influence a specific condition. He's discovered which colour to apply to which point, and in the precise sequence.

He's developed systems to treat life-threatening diseases like cancer and psychological traumas like childhood abandonment. And he's done the same for the most mundane of complaints.

Like constipation. Mine plagued me for 30 years. Until Mandel taught me to irradiate five acupuncture points with yellow, the colour of fluidity. Three points on each leg and two on each arm; ten minutes at bedtime for the following two months.

I often wonder if the laxative companies, chemical and herbal, have noticed a drop in sales.

2

Beings of light

All matter is frozen light.
David Bohm
Of Matter and Meaning: The Super-Implicate Order

In this age of pills and tablets and instant relief, is it an unfamiliar notion that light can heal? It's a concept that definitely merits reflection. Light, after all, is a prerequisite for life.

Without light no carrot would grow, no rose would bloom, no cypress stretch upwards into the sky. No robin would fly, no ant would scurry, no bullfrog croak, saluting the rain. Without light, man and the animals would disappear from the planet.

The plant kingdom is the fundamental source of food for all creatures. And it is through the process of photosynthesis, through the agency of light, that plants transform water from the earth and carbon dioxide from the air into nutrients physical bodies can metabolize and absorb. Directly or indirectly, beetroot or beefsteak, we are dining on the energy of light.

Light also influences our emotional well-being. On a bright, sunny morning we'll bounce out of bed, but if it's overcast or raining it can take all our will-power to crawl from under the covers and stagger to our feet. Sunshine cheers and invigorates. It brings a smile to our face and a spring to our step. It makes us want to tramp in the forest or head for the beach.

This positive effect of light is even reflected in our language. Don't we say 'lighten up' to someone who's down in the dumps? Or call our sweethearts the 'light' of our lives?

And why is it we so often express our emotional selves in terms of light? It is because the seat of emotions lies in the body of light that surrounds the material form – in the energy field we call the aura.[1] In this garden of light our emotions germinate and grow. And we deliver the harvest in a glance or in a caress, in a song or in a loving word.

Gross and subtle, flesh and feelings, we are manifest bodies of light.

We are also beings of light. Just as the sun is the centre of our universe, radiating its life-giving energy down on to the earth, light is also the substance of man's spirit, his soul; it is the silent inner spring from which all love, compassion and creativity flow. Mystics have been saying this for thousands of years: Buddha, Jesus, Lao Tzu, Gurdjieff, Raman Maharshi, Krishnamurti, Osho. And deep in our hearts, beyond the sway of the sceptical mind, I believe we intuitively know it to be true. When describing those who have attained this source, don't we call them 'enlightened', whatever language we speak?

Light is also our destination when we die. From *The Tibetan Book of the Dead* in the eighth century to the research of Elisabeth Kübler-Ross and Robert A. Moody Jr in the 1970s, reports of near-death experiences agree, without exception, that as we die we travel down a dark tunnel towards a realm of dazzling light. And here, in this dimension, say all those who have been and returned, we review the life we have completed, and plan what we wish to achieve in the next. Couldn't this be why we yearn for 'the light at the end of the tunnel' when we're trapped in the midst of despair?

In his book *Scriptures in Silence and Sermons in Stones*, Osho, the Indian master who attracted hundreds of thousands of Western disciples, states: 'We are born of light, we live in light, we die in light – we are made out of light. This has been one of the greatest insights of the mystics of all the ages . . .

'Now, science not only says that man is made of light but that everything is made of light; all is made of electrons, electricity. Science has come to this understanding from a very, very long route. The objective route is a very long route; the subjective route is very easy, the shortest possible, because you only have to look within.'

Or be thrown within. Which is what happened to me 20 years ago, travelling by car from Montreal towards a long weekend in New York.

It had been raining steadily for hours, the sort of early-April downpour that awakens the slumbering grasses and slicks the New York State Thruway with a slippery sheen of water. It was already dark, and my attention, carried on the headlights, was riveted on the shimmering surface ahead, focused on manoeuvring the straightest possible course between the centre line on the tarmac and the steel barrier holding back the blackness.

A radio station warned that temperatures were dropping and a night-time freeze was expected. I floored the accelerator in response, preferring to skim the liquid surface like a hydrofoil rather than skid along a freeway fast chilling to ice.

Abruptly, without warning, the car rocketed to the right, a steel barrier loomed large before me and we collided in a shattering broadside. The impact whipped the car into a second spin and it began to list, tilting into a roll. Shifting my weight corrected it, landing me on all four wheels again – but momentum had already taken over. The car flung itself against the girder again and again, the force of each collision catapulting it back for more.

Evidently it was my time to die.

I considered screaming, like in the movies, but there was no one to hear. I thought about calling on God, but knew no great hand was going to swoop down from the sky and scoop me aloft to safety.

I calculated there'd be one enormous thud, and then oblivion. I can handle that, I reckoned. So, loosening my grip on the steering wheel and folding my hands in my lap, I leaned back against the headrest, closed my eyes and said 'OK'. And meant it.

My life flashed before me on fast forward: ups and downs, successes and setbacks; milestones freezing for milliseconds on an inner screen. Then, silence. Utter and absolute. Yet this was no mere lack of noise, this was emptiness *and* fullness; this was absence teeming with presence. This silence positively pulsed with life.

My final thought, I remember, was 'This must be my soul'. Then my mind stopped, as if the plug had been pulled. And there was only space and silence where thought had been.

Still, one single point of light remained. Somewhere beyond thought a presence prevailed. And witnessing was its nature.

Then my body dissolved. Solid became molecular, as if my atomic structure had split asunder, making flesh elemental again. And where once there had been a body was nothing but light – dancing, frolicking, like fizz from champagne.

There was no sense of time; it could have been a minute, an hour, an eternity – until slowly, slowly, the sound of rain penetrated the silence, the light faded, the molecular dance subsided, and subtle was substance again. Only then were there hands and feet and a heart beating within my chest. Only then was there thinking.

As if I'd simply parked in front of my house, I stepped out on to the highway, circling the car in the driving rain. Grill mangled, headlights blind, hood buckled, the passenger side caved in. A shredded front tyre told me a blow-out had triggered the accident.

The wet and cold brought me shivering back to reality. There was a tow truck to locate, an insurance company to notify. Across the highway, beyond the steep, grassy embankment, flickered the lights of a town. Scaling the knoll, I set off across ploughed and sodden fields towards people.

Trudging through the mud, navigating by the lights in the distance, I realized something had changed inside. There'd been an arousal, a stirring, an awakening. And with it had come a shift in some fundamental perceptions.

First, I knew there was more to life than I had known up to now.

Second, I knew a silent pool of emptiness lay beyond the mind.

And third, I knew that we are beings of light.

The recognition of light as the essence of life, be it subjective or objective, is one thing. Harnessing this force to heal human ills, as Peter Mandel has done, is quite another. He is the latest pioneer in a long and illustrious tradition: mankind's efforts to heal with light are as old as recorded history.

In the temples of ancient Egypt where Ra, the sun god, was the supreme deity, special diagnostic rooms were constructed in such a way that sunlight, shining into them, was refracted into the colours of the spectrum. When the appropriate colour for treatment was identified, patients were then placed in rooms flooded with that colour. Similar practices were carried out by the early Greeks in Heliopolis, the city where Herodotus developed heliotherapy, his method of curing sickness by exposing the ill to the sun.

In modern times light-as-healer has been relegated to the dark, eclipsed by the chemicals of symptomatic medicine. This is not to say, however, that there have been no fresh inroads since the days of ancient Egypt and early Greece.

Around the turn of the last century it was found that sunlight cured bone-deforming rickets in children because Vitamin D, absorbed through the skin, triggers the body's ability to assimilate necessary calcium and phosphorus. Denmark's Niels Finsen discovered sunlight healed skin tuberculosis, winning himself a Nobel Prize in 1903. And Switzerland's Dr Auguste Rollier was awarded the same accolade for his work on phototherapy the following year.

In the decades that followed, researchers like Edwin Babbitt, Dinshah Ghadiali and Harry Riley Spitler investigated the healing properties of colour with impressive results. But the discovery of the first antibacterial sulpha drug by the Nobel Prize-winning German biochemist Gerhardt Domagk in the 1930s set medicine on a Cartesian, cause-oriented track that brought an abrupt end to any widespread interest in healing with light. Suddenly, there was an instant alternative to the more time-consuming natural methods; whatever the germ, it could now be annihilated quickly and the patient sent home, ostensibly cured.

And so mainstream medicine entered the age of symptoms, and began treating people as if their symptoms were the results of structural defects – flaws that had developed independently and in isolation, and had nothing whatever to do with the thoughts these people thought, the feelings they felt or the lives they lived. Once a symptom was no longer in evidence, it was not only out of the doctor's sight but also banished from his mind. In the years after Domagk's discovery, the occasional naturopath continued to minister with colour, but from then on, for the medical establishment, illness was basically caused by bacteria or viruses, and chemicals were the 'magic bullet' for wiping them out.

Today's overenthusiastic prescribing of antibiotics indicates that nothing much has really changed. Allopathy still views the body as a machine in which, like the cars we drive, things occasionally go wrong. Symptoms are there to be eradicated by pharmaceuticals; malfunctioning parts are replaced or removed. Even today this causal fixation continues, except that now, since we seem to be running out of new bacteria and viruses, the culprits are our genes.

The worldwide Human Genome Project, based in America, is working to analyse the structure of human DNA and to determine the location of the estimated 100,000 human genes it comprises – at a cost of 200 million dollars per year for some 15 years. The result will be a lexicon of the genetic or inherited patterns of the so-called 'average man', but how – or indeed if – science will be able to apply this generic genetic information to cure individual illnesses, or the illnesses of individuals, remains to be seen. Still, as researchers struggle to prove genetic disposition to specific conditions, to identify the gene that causes breast cancer or Aids or homosexuality or whatever, the whole man and woman – and the influence of lifestyle and conditioning on health and welfare – continues to be ignored. In many countries, unlike the UK, USA, Canada and Australia, natural medicine is officially illegal, even today.

Among allopathic doctors, there are, to be fair, those who do look beyond symptoms, who do take the lifestyles of their patients into consideration. Dr Deepak Chopra is one; Dr Bernie Siegel is another.

In his best-selling book, *Love, Medicine and Miracles,* Siegel wrote: 'Often I can suggest exactly what patients' emotional troubles are, based on the symptoms and location of their disease. Then they pour out their true feelings. After emergency surgery to remove several feet of dead intestine, a Jungian therapist recently told me, "I'm glad you're my surgeon. I've been undergoing teaching analysis. I couldn't handle all the shit that was coming up, or digest the crap in my life." Any connection with her feelings might not have occurred to another physician, but it was no coincidence to us that the intestines were the focal point of her illness. Recently after a mastectomy a woman said to me that she needed to get something off her chest.'

Zen[2] tells the story of a Chinese master who was asked by a disciple, 'What is disease?'

'Disease is a thought,' the master replied.

It appears the Chinese master wasn't kidding.

Today, the great majority of medical practitioners (the Bernie Siegels and Deepak Chopras are a rarity) still refuse to consider the individual's lifestyle as a contributing factor to illness, let alone even entertain the idea that it could be the cause! A growing number of doctors are coming to accept lifestyle as a consideration in certain ailments, like heart disease or executive stress – but, nevertheless, the unwillingness to accept the fact that man, in reality, is a unity of body, mind and spirit remains a major blind spot of Western science and, indeed, of Western civilization.

As we approach the dawn of a new century, however, times may be changing. And light, once again, may be coming into its own.

A definitive herald of this new openness is the American optometrist and phototherapist, Dr Jacob Liberman. In *Light: Medicine of the Future*, he documents the growing recognition of light and colour therapy in the treatment of a number of conditions, ranging from visual problems and learning difficulties to depression, premenstrual syndrome and certain cancers. Although he's advanced light's cause considerably by showing that symptoms do, indeed, respond to light, his focus is still *symptoms*. And a symptom is simply a clue, an outer indication of an inner disorder. What's missing is holistic; what's missing is the remembrance that we, in our essence, are beings of light.

This is the miracle and the mystery of Peter Mandel's Colourpuncture. Mandel's system treats beings of light *with* the energy of light. In my view, this makes Colourpuncture the ultimate in natural medicine.

How do we define natural medicine?

The manifesto of the British Naturopathic and Osteopathic Association describes it as 'a system of treating human ailments which recognizes that healing depends upon the vital curative force within the human organism'. The underlying hypothesis is that if the body possesses the innate capacity to heal cuts and mend fractures, then it must also be capable of resolving other disorders. Homeostasis is the term given to this self-regulating mechanism.

In relation to body functions and systems, the regulating influence of light is already well known. The part of the brain called the hypothalamus controls directly, or indirectly through the pituitary gland, a wide range of bodily functions we now know are influenced by our perception of light. The hypothalamus is energized by external light that is transformed into electrical impulses by the photoreceptors in our eyes – and, in turn, transmits regulating instructions to the pituitary, the controller of the endocrine system.

The endocrine or hormone-producing system comprises the body's circuitry of glands – pituitary, pineal, thyroid, thymus, adrenals, pancreas and gonads, the embryonic apparatus that evolves into ovaries or testes, depending on gender. This system secretes hormones into the blood for circulation throughout the body, carrying the information required to regulate many physical and chemical processes.

The autonomic nervous system, the governor of all involuntary processes like heart, gland and smooth-muscle tissue functions, is ruled by the hypothalamus – as well as the regulation of body temperature and appetite, growth and metabolism, sexual and reproductive functions, behavioural aspects like fear and rage, and the availability of 'energizers', or fuel, such as the glucose we obtain from sugars and starches, and the ATP (adenosine triphosphate) that we derive from carbohydrates.

The pineal is another endocrine gland whose function is strongly related to light. It is, for example, the body's inbuilt light meter. In response to light received from the hypothalamus, the pineal gland produces a hormone called melatonin which determines circadian rhythms,[3] setting the body's clock. Regulated by changes in the light around us, melatonin is the messenger that informs us when to sleep and when to awaken. And just as it bids a bird to moult because warm weather's on the way, it tells us it's time to try on that bathing suit to check if it's going to fit this coming summer.

For the pineal gland, however, this may be only the tip of the iceberg. In the Indian yogic tradition, the pineal gland is known as the 'third eye', the aperture on to the soul, and is also linked to the *sahasrara*, or 'crown' chakra, situated at the top of the head. This crown chakra, mystics say, is the doorway to supreme consciousness, the point of entry for the life-giving light energy emanating from the universal soul.

If light, then, is so actively involved in regulating the biochemical processes of our bodies, does it not follow that it must also play a higher, spiritual role? Many ancient cultures certainly thought so: they worshipped the sun and its healing rays, and viewed light as the carrier of a subtle, nourishing energy they credited with being the source of life itself.

Samuel Hahnemann, the founder of homoeopathy, called this energy 'the vital curative force'. He said that it is not only the regulating and balancing force which keeps us healthy, but it is also the very energy that gives us life. In different traditions and disciplines, it is known by different names. It is the *prana* of the Hindus, the *iliaster* of Paracelsus, the *nefish* of the Jewish Kabbalah, the *orgone* energy of Wilhelm Reich.

Chinese medicine calls this life force *ch'i* – and as far back as 3000 BC Chinese physicians identified a network of invisible paths or energy 'meridians' in the body through which the *ch'i* is carried to the cells of tissues and organs. Along these meridians they identified more than one thousand points or portals on the skin through which the *ch'i* is absorbed into the body. They further discovered that particular points relate to specific body organs and functions, and that the condition of these internal organs or processes can be influenced via these points.

The most widely practised means for restoring the unimpeded flow of *ch'i* is through needles inserted at these acupuncture points. The needles either stimulate or impede the flow of energy, depending on the course required to re-establish balance and, therefore, restore health.

In their efforts to return their patients to a state of health and equilibrium, colour practitioners Edwin Babbitt and Dinshah

Ghadiali shone light on large sections of the body through coloured filters, while Harry Riley Spitler (like Dr Jacob Liberman today) introduced light through the eyes. Peter Mandel's Colourpuncture, however, irradiates acupuncture points – and other meridian systems – with focused applications of coloured light.

The decision to irradiate points on the skin instead of large areas was a conscious one for Mandel, and in 1989 he received substantial affirmation that his hunch had been right. At the Institute for Clinical and Experimental Medicine in Nowosibirsk, then part of the Soviet Union, a research team led by one Professor Kaznachejew proved that there exist, in the body, channels of light corresponding to the meridians of traditional Chinese medicine, and that the sectors of the body which take in light match the acupuncture points precisely!

In my view, this makes Colourpuncture a true medicine of light for we beings of light. Streaming down these channels, heading straight for the cells, Colourpuncture beams the healing, regulating information embodied in the natural energy of light – addressing the imbalance we call sickness and restoring the harmony we define as health.

Our intelligent cells

On both an energetic and a spiritual level, man is a being of light – and the same essential quality can be attributed to our cells. At the International Institute of Biophysics in Kaiserslautern, in Germany, Dr Fritz-Albert Popp has proved that the cells of all living things radiate light. In other words, light is present in every cell of our bodies. It is extremely faint, Popp says, and corresponds to the intensity of a candle flame seen from a distance of some 25 kilometres.

This radiation from living cells – or 'biophoton emission', as he terms it – represents a regulating energy field that encompasses the entire organism and exerts an essential influence on all the body's biochemical processes. In biological systems, photons participate in all atomic and molecular interactions, and the word 'biophoton' has been coined to emphasize that the photon emission from living organisms carries bio-information relating to bodily processes. And the function of this biophoton emission is, in Popp's own words, 'intra- and intercellular regulation and communication'.

The fact that our cells possess the ability to communicate presupposes the existence of cellular intelligence – and in advanced scientific circles this reality is already acknowledged.

In *Quantum Healing* Dr Deepak Chopra discusses how cellular intelligence manifests in the cells of our DNA. He explains how the DNA in the nucleus of each cell is 'constantly bathed in a swirl of free-floating organic molecules, the basic building blocks of the material body', and that, when it wishes to form new DNA, it attracts the specific chemicals it requires.

'The DNA knows exactly what information to pick out and how it all goes together for each thing it wants to "say" chemically,' Chopra writes. 'Besides building itself, DNA knows how to build RNA, or ribonucleic acid, which is nearly its identical twin and active counterpart. RNA's mission is to travel away from the DNA in order to produce the proteins, more than two million in number, that actually build and repair the body . . .

'DNA does not work just from rote memory. It can invent new chemicals at will (such as a new antibody after you catch a strain of flu you have never been exposed to before).'

One particular experiment of Popp's not only confirms that intelligence exists in every living cell, but also illustrates clearly that light is, indeed, the language of the cells.

In this procedure, using a photomultiplier,[4] a red light quantum was radiated on to a cell, and it replied with a beam in the blue spectrum. The significance is that 'blue' was an *answer*, and not simply a reflection. Had it been a reflection, the response would have been red or, at least, its complementary colour, green. This was no mirroring; 'blue' was a definite reply.

In *Energia Vitale*, a documentary shown in 1995 on Swiss-Italian television, again with the help of a photomultiplier, Popp visibly demonstrated this cellular communication at work. He showed that cells talk to each other via light impulses – just like ships at sea communicate with the dots and dashes of Morse code transposed into short and long bursts of light.

In the 1990s, in developed countries, whenever we pick up the telephone we, too, are also communicating with light. All over the world, connecting city to city and country to country over terrestrial and submarine installations, more than ninety-six million kilometres of optical fibre telecommunications networks transmit voice, image, video and data through impulses of light.

Encased in a sleeve of glass as fine as gossamer and smaller than a human hair, light is the core of a fibre-optic cable. A telephone conversation, for example, is digitally decoded into light vibrations and pulsed to its destination. On arrival at its destination, it is decoded into the caller's voice once again. And the capacity of a single beam of light is staggering: one optical fibre cable can carry 200,000 telephone conversations simultaneously!

If it is true that there is nothing new under the sun, that no knowledge is ever lost but stored in some Akashic record or Rupert Sheldrake-like morphic field,[5] then this use of light as a vehicle of communication may be simply a replica, on a social and planetary level, of the very system already used by our cells.

What is it, then, that living cells communicate in their language of light?

'The experimental results collected and the theoretical considerations so far make it probable that biophotons are carrying bio-information in connection with physiological processes of biological systems,' wrote W P Mei, an associate of Popp's, in the *Journal of Biological Systems*.[6]

And how can we learn to decipher what is being said?

At the institute in Kaiserslautern, Popp has developed a means for measuring the biophoton emission of beings and plants, and in experiments documented in his most recent book, *Die Botschaft der Nahrung* (The Message of Food), he demonstrates the marked difference in the biophoton emission – and nourishment content – of foods grown by natural methods.

We're all familiar with the difference in taste and the feeling of sustenance we get from eating organic, vine-ripened tomatoes. Over a year-long study, Popp and a team of fourteen researchers proved that tomatoes grown by biological methods displayed twice the biophoton emission of those grown by hydroponics – and that those grown conventionally, with chemical fertilizers, showed approximately one-fifth less the biophoton emission of the organic tomatoes.

The same dramatic results characterized a study of egg production. Free-range eggs registered twice the amount of biophoton emissions than those laid by battery chickens imprisoned in cages. And emissions were even higher when the weather was sunny!

In addition, Popp found that the use of preservatives drastically reduced the biophoton emission. Twenty-eight sunflower oils were measured, and their ability to store light was virtually lost when the oil had been refined.

From these tests, Popp is learning to understand the language of biophotons. He has been able to infer that the ability of a plant to transmit the information we need for optimum nutrition – directly, or indirectly via animal products – is dependent on the plant's ability to absorb and store light. We are not only sustained by the substances in food, but also from this stored light. We not only ingest calories, vitamins, proteins and minerals, but the entire bio-information of the plant and, indeed, the complete life information of any animal we eat.

The healing powers of the bio-information contained in healthy, organically grown plants was also the focal point of the work of the late German-born scientist Werner Kropp. Kropp claimed to have developed a technology – which he named Energetic Resonance and Interference Technology (ERIT) – that 'restores balance in active biological systems by transferring bio-information from healthy plants, thus completing missing information content and activating self-healing powers'. The bio-information is carried in a 'biotransmitter', such as water or oil, and the cell system, Kropp stated, only picks up information which is missing or which it needs in order to function properly – further evidence of cellular intelligence.

Before his death in February 1995, Verena and I spent time with Werner Kropp at his laboratory near Locarno, in Switzerland. 'Biological systems function on the basis of energetic information transmitted via ultra-faint electric currents,' he told us, reinforcing Popp's findings that light is the language of the cells. 'Disturbances in the electric climate of a cell lead to disease or degeneration of the cells. To restore healing the natural milieu must be established; that means the energetic information has to be corrected.

'Only the body can heal itself through its own biological system,' he added, echoing an insight we'd heard from Mandel on several occasions. 'All the help a therapist can give is to support the self-healing process of the body. The more natural this activation of self-healing forces, the faster illness or malfunction is eradicated.'

In his Wekroma brand of products, widely used by European naturopaths, Kropp imprinted this bio-information, this 'stored light', on harmless carriers (like water and oil and powdered rock) for ingestion or for external application, whereas Mandel, through his Colourpuncture system, imparts to the body, directly, the informative energies inherent in the colours of light.

Whether mankind will ever fully decode what one cell is saying by 'red' and another is answering by 'blue' remains to be seen, but close attention and observation, over thousands of years, has revealed certain indications about the message individual colours convey.

In his *Farbenlehre* (The Theory of Colour), published in 1840, Johann Wolfgang von Goethe, the great German poet and philosopher, set forth his view of colour as a living entity of spiritual significance, and stressed the importance of experiencing colour as a vital energy of life.

Goethe's hypothesis exerted a strong influence on the Swiss occultist, religious leader and educator Rudolph Steiner. Convinced, through his own extensive research, of the influence of colours on the emotions that rule our actions, Steiner predicted a major therapeutic role for colour in the coming age.

The seed that Goethe planted took root in other fertile minds. And over the years, in healing circles, the body of knowledge grew. For purposes of illustration, let us briefly look at some of the therapeutic capabilities documented for Goethe's three primary colours, red, blue and yellow.

Red, 'the father of vitality', is said to exert a cheering effect and to arouse passion. Red is also known to stimulate circulation and, because the blood is the carrier of the immune cells, is therefore indicated in the treatment of various wounds and inflammations.

Yellow symbolizes the mind and the intellect, and has been seen to foster learning and understanding in children. It is also the colour of movement and fluidity and, as such, is used to promote digestion, stimulate the stomach and liver, and strengthen the ebb and flow of the glandular and nerve systems.

Blue is the colour of inspiration, devotion, peace and tranquillity. A cool colour, it is indicated for lowering fever, reducing pain, relieving congestion, and is used in alleviating insomnia, shocks and headaches.

It was Goethe who discovered that these three primary colours are the basis of all colours, and that any colour can be produced by mixing these three.

In the hands of a Claude Monet or a Vincent Van Gogh, these primary colours have been transmuted into unimagined hues and, with brush and canvas, transformed into images that communicate the vision of the heart, the eye of the soul. With his palette of light, Peter Mandel's art is equally inspiring. He has harnessed the colours of the rainbow to heal his fellow man, regulating the disharmonies that make him ill and lighting his way on the path towards wholeness.

3

Who's that knocking?

There must be something I can do better than anyone.
PETER BLAKELEY
Harry's Café de Wheels

There is an in-between realm where certain people live, a kind of twilight zone where frontiers overlap and dimensions mingle. It's a place where worlds collide – where the unseen penetrates the seen; where auras and auguries, visions and visitations are as run-of-the-mill as breathing.

Some are born to transcendence, to this twofold state. Others achieve it through meditation. Then there are those who have it thrust upon them through illness or accident. Like Peter Mandel. He was five and a half when he died and came back to life.

For two months, however, he lay in a coma, floating in limbo, and when his eyes finally opened it was on to a new reality – one that was isolating to inhabit and impossible to share because a fundamental shift had taken place. He found himself in the world yet no more of it; things were still what they were yet no longer what they seemed. And when he finally realized he was different, all he wanted was to be the same.

'I completely blocked out the experience,' he said to Verena and me in the book-lined den of his home in Wiesloch, a stone's throw from the ancient university town of Heidelberg. All he'd known was what he'd been told: he'd suffered a near-fatal mishap as a youngster. And the fact that pounding headaches plagued his days and a recurring nightmare robbed his sleep – well, that was just how it was. For almost two decades, his constant companions were confusion and pain.

At 18, triggered by a chance encounter in a tavern, the incident he'd managed to bury suddenly burst upon his consciousness again: he remembered leaving his body and travelling down a cavernous tunnel; he remembered a brilliant light beckoning from the other end.

There, in that crowded tavern, an inner window, darkly shuttered until now, flew open. And, carried on the light of memory, understanding flooded in. 'I had forgotten that as a child, after the accident, I was always roaming in other dimensions,' he told us. 'And it is still like this. In a way, I am absent: I am here but I am not. But I somehow know if this death hadn't happened, I wouldn't be doing what I am right now.'

The event that rewrote the script of Peter Mandel's life occurred in 1947, in Wipfeld, a farming community of 800 nestled on the river Main in the wine-growing region between Schweinfurt and Würzburg.

On the day in question, Peter Mandel and his best friends, Anton and Manfred, met at their usual spot in front of Manfred's house before heading off to play in the fields where their mothers were working. 'We were always ravenous,' Mandel recalled, 'and we could usually count on the farmers for a handful of berries, a slice of sausage, or a chunk of freshly baked bread smothered in home-made jam.' But this particular afternoon they were distracted en route: the village carpenter had finally finished the shelves for the new pharmacy. He was nowhere in sight, and the stack of shelves, ten metres high, simply begged to be climbed. Mandel was the first to scale the top.

In the cottage opposite, Manfred's father Hans heard a thunderous crash mingled with the frightened cries of children. Running to the window, he saw a cloud of dust billowing from the workshop doorway – and there, seconds later, he found the three boys buried under a jumble of broken shelves. His own son was shaken but unhurt, yet the other two had not been so lucky: Anton had cut his face badly and young Peter had split his skull. Motionless, the boy lay on the earthen floor in a spreading pool of blood. As neighbours arrived to look to the others, Hans fashioned a makeshift bandage about Peter's head and, lifting him carefully, set out for the pea harvest to find Mrs Mandel.

Like a grass fire fanned by the wind, news of the accident flashed to the fields, and by the time she sighted Hans in the distance Helene Mandel already knew something serious had happened to her younger son. But it wasn't until they got him to the nearby military hospital and the doctors removed the blood-soaked bandage that she realized the gravity of his condition. The right side of his skull had sustained a massive fracture, a rusty nail was embedded in the temple, the eye had been dislodged and fluid from the brain was oozing out from behind the gaping socket.

The doctors operated immediately, repairing the damage as best they could. But they offered no hope. 'Take the boy home, Mrs Mandel,' they told her. 'And when he dies, be happy, because if he survives he will certainly be retarded.'

The doctors didn't know Helene Mandel. She'd already been through too much to bring her two sons this far. And this small one, she vowed silently, was going to live. Her boys were all she had left from her former life in Schlesien. Now part of Poland, it then belonged to Germany – and the Nazis had taken everything else away.

The daughter of the assistant postmaster general in what is today the Polish town of Breslau, Helene had married late. Doctors had told her she would never bear children, but the auto-worker Erich August Mandel, several years her junior, loved her and said he really didn't mind. But they had been wrong – as she now determined these army doctors would also be – and in 1938 she gave birth to a son, Eberhard, and then, in 1941, to Peter. A year later she was a widow, her husband killed at the front. With two babies to feed and precious little to put into their bellies, she decided to make her way to the village on the Main, where her mother had settled some time before.

It was the winter of 1945, there was a war on, and it was a long, hard trek. Helene Mandel travelled by foot and cart and train, her boys protected against the cold in coats she'd fashioned from scraps of Russian rugs. But in the Dresden railway station came the final blow. When Peter suddenly crawled under the locomotive for warmth, and she dropped her suitcases to run to rescue him, her bags were stolen – and with them their remaining possessions. When she finally stumbled into Wipfeld, toes burning from frostbite, they had nothing left, not even a spoon.

Yet she'd managed. And she'd spent too many back-breaking hours toiling in the fields for a loaf of bread or a slab of sausage to lose this little one now.

Her determined optimism infected a local country physician and his son, also a doctor. Between them, buoyed by Helene Mandel's indomitable will, they maintained a round-the-clock vigil beside the boy's bed. It was to be a long eight weeks of touch-and-go before he awoke from his coma.

As we spoke of this in his study at Wiesloch, Mandel suddenly grew reflective. 'Something quite mysterious happened at this time, but I only know of it from others,' he said quietly. 'Apparently the old doctor and his son were at my bedside when the young man was called to another patient. A half-hour later I awoke from the coma – and at that very moment he was killed in a car crash. Somehow, inside, I sense a correlation, but I don't understand it. I often used to wonder if perhaps one had to go so the other could stay.'

Cosmic connection or pure coincidence, this was the first of many such incidents to mark Mandel's life. Somehow he always managed to pick up the book he needed to read, be somewhere he needed to be, or come across someone he needed to meet – after, that is, he finally acknowledged the new world he inhabited. Trying to ignore it, he learned the hard way, brought nothing but pain.

He was between seven and eight when the headaches began. At night they were so severe his own screams would awaken him; during the day they often took him to the edge of unconsciousness. From his present perspective he believes they started because he stopped accepting his own reality.

'As a child I used to tell stories the whole day long,' he said. 'I would sit in the garden and watch the sap rising in the poplar trees, or I would see fairies in the forest or gnomes in the hay barn – and I would come home and tell my mother, always emphatic that what I'd seen was real. It used to embarrass her, particularly if other people were around, and she would say, "Don't listen to the little one. Pay no attention: he's just crazy again." So I stopped saying anything. And that's when the headaches started.'

Then there was the recurring dream. 'There was always a grey fog and a sound, a kind of knocking.' With his knuckle he struck the coffee table between us: Tok! Tok! Tok! His rap was firm, insistent. 'Like that,' he said.

'This noise persecuted me the whole time, night and day. It influenced the entire quality of my life. I couldn't concentrate on anything, and it affected my schoolwork so badly that by the third year in the gymnasium I failed the exam and had to repeat the term. But I didn't care: I had completely lost interest in doing anything.'

'It sounds as if life was trying to tell you something,' I offered, 'like it was knocking loud and long to get your attention.'

'That could well be,' he chuckled. 'But at the time I obviously wasn't ready to answer the door.'

There was always a price for not listening: another hit on the head. Peter Mandel got concussions like other kids got scraped knees. A football in the face, a fall from a bicycle, a dive into shallow water, a fracas with other boys – there was always another concussion. And more headaches.

Today, it's obvious: he damaged himself whenever he avoided, whenever he tried to ignore the inner world that kept insisting on being acknowledged.

The child is father to the man, they say. And here, in this childhood besieged by pain, we see the first stirrings of the kind of man Peter Mandel grew to be.

He has tremendous compassion for others who are hurting. And whenever a patient comes to his practice in distress and discomfort, the first thing Mandel does is administer a treatment to relieve the pain.

'It took me many years to realize that pain is a message, that it is the body's way of telling us that somewhere, in some aspect of our life, something is amiss,' he said. 'But before people can accept this; before they can see, with any semblance of clarity, whatever it is they're trying to avoid or suppress, they have to stop hurting.

'The latest American research shows that there is no isolated pain centre in the brain, that when pain occurs it floods the entire brain. This reinforces my own observation. From years of first-hand experience I know that pain is all-consuming, that it is utterly overwhelming, that it leaves no room for reflection or introspection, for trying to figure out, "Why is this happening to me?" First, I try to ease the pain of those who come to me. In this way, we create a space for their innate wisdom to surface, for their own being to tell them why the pain is there, and what is causing it.'

This insight – that pain is life's messenger – is rarely part of a modern medical discipline; it's more commonly found in therapy, in group work, and is generally accompanied by an understanding that the source of pain, physical or psychological, lies in some past traumatic event or experience. Most people, however, still view the cause of pain or suffering as external, as outside themselves, as an undeserved torment inflicted by an uncaring existence.

Whatever the patient's attitude, whether there's an acceptance of pain as life's messenger or a total rejection of the possibility, Colourpuncture sets the healing process in motion.

Its route is from below to above, from lower to higher, from bottom to top. Colourpuncture begins its work in the depths of our beings, with the very consciousness in our cells. Through the agency of light, energy that has been blocked by shock or trauma is released, and the newly freed consciousness begins its voyage upwards, traversing the levels of emotion and intellect until, at last, with an 'Aha!' of conscious awareness, the light of understanding dawns.

Esogetic medicine and Colourpuncture are the result of years of thought and theory, dedicated testing and re-testing, of extremely long hours and tremendously hard work. And for this stamina, for this sense of dedication and purpose, Peter Mandel thanks his mother.

At nine, he remembers complaining to her that he never had pocket money like other kids. She had no ideas to offer, simply forthright advice: 'If you want money, then earn it.' So he opened a shop. He sold tiny mounds of peas and lentils and spoonfuls of flour, and everyone in the family *had* to buy. Or with a little straw basket strapped to his back he'd venture into the forest to collect twigs and bark for cooking fuel. Or he'd gather lilies of the valley, fashion them into bouquets, and sell them door-to-door.

'I loved selling, the exchange, the give and take,' he told us. 'I saw that if I sell something I get something, and then I can buy something from somebody, and they can do the same. I was never interested in being rich, and very early in life I learned not to hold on to money: I saw that money's an energy, that it needs to circulate. And I'm grateful to my mother because she created the opportunity for me to find this out for myself.'

Respect for work came harder: it began at 15 when his mother apprenticed him to a job he didn't want. Times were tough, she said, and he'd better be grateful for whatever he could get. For the next three years Mandel laboured as a fitter in a foundry. He was tall for his age, and strong, and his first task was beating iron all day long in front of a red-hot forge. 'It was an incredible horror,' he shuddered, 'and one day I simply walked out. I went home and said "I can't do this any more."' But his mother wouldn't buy it. She led him back to work, spoke to the manager and had him transferred to another department. The family needed the money.

His only relief was partying. And he dived into escape with a single-minded vengeance, into beer and spirits and carousing till the wee small hours. One morning, about five, he staggered home drunk, and when six-thirty came and his mother tried to awaken him for work, he immediately began to vomit. Helene Mandel had

had enough. Shaking with anger, she hurled a wet floor rag into his face. 'Anyone who can drink can also work,' she shouted.

It shocked him, that he'd driven her to this. Embarrassed, he looked away, out of the window, anywhere but into her eyes. And then he remembered.

Six months after he surfaced from the coma, just able to crawl, he was at the window watching his mother chopping wood in the yard. All at once the axe slipped and she almost lopped off her thumb. 'It was hanging by a bit of skin,' he said. 'I watched her put it back in place, clutch it tightly to her bosom and run down the street towards the pharmacy. The chemist told her to forget the thumb, to cut if off and just throw it away. "Not on your life," she said to him. "I want it to stay." And it did. She took such good care of it, it grew back together. There was a big scar and it was a bit crooked, but later she could use it like any normal thumb.

'This was a very important lesson for me, seeing her strength, her incredible will. And I never forgot it. In later years, no matter when I got to bed, or in what condition, I was always at work on time the next morning. And when I began giving seminars and was still into lots of beer and little sleep, I was there with total energy every time and nobody ever knew the difference.'

Meanwhile, he was still trapped in the foundry. And then, one day, the rivet gun got him in the forehead. 'I woke up in the hospital again,' he said, fingering a scar curving upwards above his right eyebrow. 'Another concussion.'

But it wasn't quite the last straw. That came when a co-worker suggested they finagle six weeks off with sick pay by shooting themselves with the nail gun. 'I hear it doesn't hurt at all,' he said. And then he pulled the trigger and a nail tore through his hand.

'Something flipped in me in that moment,' Mandel said. 'I simply couldn't function in this kind of numbing, self-destructive environment any longer.'

'And what do you intend to do now?' his mother asked when he told her he'd quit. 'You haven't learned any profession.'

'I'm going into military service,' he replied. 'Maybe there I can learn something.'

He signed up for four years. He was to report to the Munich barracks on 1 July 1959, two weeks after his 18th birthday.

That year, his birthday party was also his send-off. Around three in the morning Mandel and his mates decided to stop by the bar of the local sporting club for one last drink. And there, sitting in the corner, was Hans, the father of his childhood friend Manfred.

He was instantly sober. 'And I knew I absolutely must talk to this man. It was as if my very life depended on it.' Pulling up a chair, he sat down. 'Do you remember me?'

Hans nodded. 'Little Peter Mandel.'

'I am at a crossroads right now,' he blurted, his voice quaking. 'My life is changing: one part is over and another is just beginning, and I have to ask you to explain to me what happened back then. But first I want to tell you about a dream I have again and again.'

Huddled over the table in the noisy bar, he told his rescuer about the nightmare, about the grey fog and the sound that had haunted him for so long. Over the passing years the fog had lifted bit by bit until he could see that there was a man in the dream and that he was carrying someone in his arms. 'I know you were that man and that it was me you were carrying, but what was that sound? It's been torturing me for as long as I can remember. Were you wearing boots with nails or something?'

'No,' Hans replied, 'but maybe it was your blood dropping on the road. It left a trail through the village anyone could follow.'

In that moment a veil lifted from Mandel's eyes. And for the first time pictures came: leaving his body as the shelves tumbled; watching the scene from above; travelling down a long, dark tunnel with a light at the end. And at last he understood what had happened. He had died and come back to life.

It frightened and fascinated him. And it triggered a shift in consciousness. 'This was the first big kick in starting me thinking in a new direction. Up to then I paid no attention to concepts like God, or life after death, or anything remotely spiritual. Suddenly, I found myself pondering these mysteries.

'I've never spoken of this before,' he continued after a brief moment in which I was aware of being assessed. 'It was then I began to realize that if I had indeed come back, there must be some reason for it. But what, I had no idea.'

In the army now

On 1 July 1959 Peter Mandel donned the uniform of the West German army. On 2 July he knew he'd made a terrible mistake. He'd stepped from one frying pan into another; this was as mindless as the foundry. But he'd signed up for a long stretch. So, for the next four years, he spent more time malingering than marching, more time in trouble than out of it.

The encounter with Hans had kindled a flame. But only for a moment. All his life he'd managed to escape, and now, in the army, he continued to do the same.

Bucking the bosses became the name of the game. He learned how to bend the rules to have a good time. 'But my friends and I overestimated ourselves. We always got caught.'

Between 1959 and 1963 Mandel was reprimanded 11 times, for all sorts of escapades – from insubordination and ignoring NATO alarms to drunkenness and street brawls, from damaging military property to trading in army goods, from forging driving orders for a visit to Munich to making a spontaneous detour to his mother's house in Wipfeld on the way to a field exercise.

Things were picking up, however. During this time he only had one concussion. He'd borrowed a new car with only 500 kilometres on the tachometer and, as he put it, 'drove it into scrap metal'. It was his fault and he had to pay. But, as usual, he had no money. And, as she always did, his mother came to the rescue. Without blame or question she simply went to the bank and took out a loan. 'You'll be the death of me some day, my boy,' she muttered, handing over the cash.

I got the impression it quite surprised him, but lying there in the hospital bed, recovering from his latest concussion, a new direction for his energies began to take shape, albeit tentatively, in Peter Mandel's mind. He decided to become a medical orderly, and when he finished basic training he was sent to school in a military hospital in Giessen, just north of Frankfurt.

As it transpired, however, he wasn't quite ready for schooling yet. An American garrison was also stationed in Giessen, and the playground for the boys of both armies was nearby Hessen, a village of lovely girls, lively beer halls and lucrative games of chance. But Mandel and his pals were always penniless, so one of his mates proposed a solution. Somewhere along the line Mandel had learned to yodel passably well, and his chum, posing as his manager, sweet-talked the owner of the busiest tavern in town into food and drinks in exchange for Mandel's Alpine melodies.

And it was there, from the stage of the *Oberbayern*, clad in the traditional Bavarian costume of leather shorts and a plumed hat, that one night, in mid-yodel, 19-year-old Peter Mandel looked down into the audience and fell in love. Her name was Christine and she was from East Germany.

The next four months, he said, were the happiest he'd ever known. Then, with that particular rudeness that often characterizes reality, his training was suddenly over and he was transferred back to Munich. Then Christine called: she was pregnant. Together they travelled to Wipfeld to tell Helene Mandel that not only was her son getting married, but she was also going to be a grandmother.

But a life together wasn't on the cards. One day, without a word, Christine was simply gone, back east to the Deutsche Demokratische Republik, the DDR. He wrote and phoned and went to see her, but she wouldn't budge: Christine intended to raise her baby in a world she knew.

He was 19, and the loss devastated him. He dived into drinking and gambling with renewed vengeance – and into another short-lived affair. And soon another infant was on the way.

His mother, he said, was not too pleased with her profligate son, but she lived to see Mandel reunited with these two children. And had she lived longer, Helene Mandel would have watched Martina and Markus follow in their father's footsteps, becoming successful naturopaths and Colourpuncturists in their own right.

The emotional turmoil of Christine's abrupt departure provoked an increase in the frequency and severity of Mandel's headaches – and the army medics stepped in. Their examination revealed an osteoma, a bone cyst, behind the right eye. This could well be the cause of the headaches. It had best be removed.

The procedure was new – cutting open the eyebrow, drilling into the bone, dislodging the eye from its socket and then going in behind to extract the cyst – but it could only be performed under a local anaesthetic; a general was too dangerous.

They were four hours of hell. 'The noises were the worst,' Mandel said, visibly wincing at the memory. 'On top of the incessant drilling, there was a clock on the wall with a minute hand that beat out the same awful rhythm as in my dream. It was an absolute horror. And it changed nothing: the headaches went on, the same as before.'

Another change, however, was just around the corner.

Into a tavern one evening strolled another young woman. Her name was Anna, and she could have been Christine's twin. Peter Mandel fell in love all over again.

And he stopped drinking. Which was timely, because he suddenly received a summons to see his commanding officer. Even though he only had six months left to serve, the army was seriously considering tossing him out with a dishonourable discharge. The alternatives were straightforward: mend his ways or risk his demobilization pay.

The threat triggered a 180-degree turn. 'I knew I couldn't keep on living like this,' Mandel said. 'I saw that if I kept on, I would turn out to be a bum. And I didn't want that. I wanted to *be* someone.

'Everything flipped, and with a speed that still amazes me today. It was as if someone had turned a key in my head and said, "OK, this is finished now, from now on it's a new ball game." I couldn't drink any more; I couldn't go out in the evenings. I started to read, whatever I could get my hands on.

'And I got married.' He paused for a moment, then added shyly, 'But this time I didn't *have* to.'

Something nobody else has done

His army mates could hardly believe that this young man who lay on his bunk night after night for the next six months, lost in a book, was the same Peter Mandel. They watched the number of books he consumed, and the rate at which he devoured them, and said it simply wasn't possible anyone could read that much, that fast. But Mandel had had a talent for photographic reading since childhood, and no matter how they tried to trick him out, no matter which book, page or line they selected, he could quote the passage accurately. It became, he said, one of his 'seminar tricks' when he began teaching Colourpuncture in later years.

Although he read anything and everything, from fairy tales and folklore to detective and westerns, he had a particular passion for archaeology and science fiction, for books about a world that was and a world that could be.

Ancient Egypt thrilled him most. 'I still can't explain it, but I had this overwhelming feeling I was reading about a time that had something to do with me,' he said. 'Years afterwards, whenever I visited Paris, I was always drawn to the Egyptian section at the Louvre. Every time I found something special, some image or sculpture that touched me and made its influence felt later on.'

With only six months left in uniform, when he wasn't working or reading he was planning his future. He was already a trained nurse, he had good hands, and one evening he had the sudden idea he'd like to do therapeutic massage. One of his first acts as a civilian was to enrol in the State Massage School of the University of Heidelberg. It was 1964.

Being a full-time student was one thing, but he also had a newly pregnant wife. And, remembering his mother – 'If you want to have money, then earn it' – he placed a newspaper ad for night work.

For the next year, Mandel reckons he slept an average of two hours a day. He would get home from his night job at around six in the morning, shower, eat breakfast, go to school from eight till one, study for two hours and then sleep until it was time to go back to work at five. At last, he often used to think, the training of his dissolute teens was coming in handy.

Finally, his studies came to an end and Mandel graduated among the top three in his class. Money, however, was still an issue. Ahead of him lay a long period of probation, and with it, an ongoing shortage of funds. Then opportunity knocked. A modern physiotherapy clinic was to be built at a Catholic hospital in Heidelberg, and the nuns were looking for someone to run it. Ignoring the fact that he had no experience, Peter applied. 'I told them I was young and dynamic, and would do a fantastic job!'

As part of the screening process, each applicant was given a blueprint of the proposed facility and asked for suggestions. Mandel took his copy to an architectural planner he knew. 'If you were building this clinic,' he asked, 'what improvements would you make?'

Considering the plans for a few moments, his friend pointed to the taps and drains in the bathing station. 'Look how small these are,' he said. 'Now, calculate how much time it's going to take to fill these tubs, empty them and then refill them again. If you double the size of the taps and drains, you can handle twice the number of patients in the same amount of time. And generate twice the money.'

Mandel was impressed. So were the nuns. Enough to give him the job, at the same starting salary as a head physician. 'Look, I no sooner graduate from school than I'm a director!' he boasted when he came home with the news.

He dived totally into his new career and by the third quarter had realized the profit the hospital had projected for the end of the second year. But in his drive to succeed, he trampled on some toes.

The women who tended the baths were constantly going to the Mother Superior to complain that Mandel-said-this or Mandel-did-that, and he was regularly summoned to justify himself. By the end of 1967 he'd had enough.

And then, one November afternoon, a corpulent gentleman mounted his massage table. 'With your talents I'd be working for myself,' the man said halfway through the session. 'I have the perfect spot for you, in the best part of Heidelberg.'

It was ideal. It would make a very classy clinic indeed. The only problem was the rent: an unaffordable 680 marks a month. But he wanted his independence badly, and Mandel-the-gambler signed on the spot. 'Then there was the problem of going home to tell my wife we were giving up a secure existence for one she was bound to think of as insecure, as well as an utterly arrogant move on my part.'

Anna nearly fell off her chair. Was he mad? There was his son and his new baby daughter to feed! And she'd just finished furnishing their new apartment! Within moments she was on the phone to Helene Mandel, and the next morning, bright and early, his mother was at the front door. He'd heard her stomping down the hallway, muttering and grumbling, before she even reached their flat.

'My mother started carrying on as if the world were collapsing and everyone was going to starve,' Mandel grinned. 'But I said, "OK, I'll prove to you once again that I can still earn a lot of money without having an ordinary job. I've done it before and I'll do it again."'

The new Mandel Institute for Spine and Joint Disorders was an overnight success. He was the hottest masseur in Heidelberg. And he was always booked out.

To all intents and purposes, Peter Mandel finally had everything: a home and family, satisfying work, a booming business. But deep down inside, where it really matters, there still smouldered the fire of discontent. He sensed something trying to surface, some force floundering for expression. He felt it had to do with dying and coming back, with why he had been spared, yet nothing was clear. All he knew right now was that he wanted to make as much money as he possibly could.

He'd always been enterprising, even as a child in Wipfeld, selling lilies of the valley from door to door – and from this moment on, throughout Peter Mandel's life, innovation and success were to walk hand in hand. 'I remember telling myself: to earn more money, you have to do something other people don't do. It was a very significant realization; it was the spark that ignited my engine. Up to that point, this was the most important impulse of my life.

'Looking back, however, money was just the excuse. There was this inner drive to do something no one else did. At first, when people ridiculed my ideas about Kirlian diagnosis and treating with Colourpuncture, this urge to do something no one else did was what gave me the courage to go on.'

It also pushed him to do things better. And incentives weren't lacking. Just as in his Bruchsal clinic today, the majority of the people who visited the Heidelberg practice in the late 1960s were people who'd been everywhere else before and couldn't be helped. Second, his treatments weren't covered by insurance but had to be paid for in cash. Not only did these factors lift his patients' expectations, they also raised Mandel's expectations of himself.

This put a strain on him I think he actually enjoyed. He was only truly satisfied if a patient walked away free of pain. And this was happening more and more frequently – although he could rarely say why.

Putkammer and Cornelius, a pair of well-known German therapeutic masseurs, had already demonstrated the gradual healing effect of massage on Chinese acupuncture points. But what Mandel had begun to notice was that pressure on certain points was bringing *immediate* relief from pain. In case after case, pain was suddenly gone; pressure on a certain point had simply taken it away. 'I was obviously doing something right, although I wasn't exactly sure what,' he said. Determined to find out, he began to observe the reactions of his patients very closely. And he began to keep very detailed notes.

When people came with sciatica, for example, he saw that if he applied pressure on specific points, on points that had no apparent connection whatsoever with the protrusion of the nerve from the spine, the pain was instantly gone – even when a follow-up examination revealed the nerve still pinched between the vertebrae. He concluded the logical: the trapped nerve alone could not be the cause of the pain. It wasn't until later that he began to suspect a connection between emotional stress and spinal disorders.

But at the time, as Mandel put it: 'The problem was that all these conclusions were theoretical or only described correlations. Nobody ever said, "If you press here, this happens." And that's what I was looking for.'

An answer finally came. At least, an answer of sorts. And it didn't come from a book or from anyone else's research.

One night at about eleven, driving home from the clinic, the first complete system of his very own was suddenly there, as clear as a bell, as if a light had gone on in his head.

He pulled over, walked to the closest tavern, ordered a beer and spent the next 20 minutes mulling over the insight. 'It was the first time in my life everything fell into place so quickly and easily. Just before midnight I went home and started writing it down. By two in the morning, I had the first complete system of my very own – points, sequence, everything. It was for treating spine and shoulder complaints, migraines and sciatic pain, by massaging certain acupuncture points on the body.

'I tried it out and it worked – as I somehow knew it would. And it deepened my trust in my own abilities.'

It also heightened his dissatisfaction.

There was never time to ponder the questions that nagged him. He was earning 'enormous amounts' of money, but working 'like a horse', 16 to 17 hours a day. And still the headaches came and went – simply irritating at times; at others, so bad he almost fainted.

It wasn't so much the work or the headaches – he'd somehow learned to handle both – it was mostly the restriction, the feeling confined. He wanted to experiment, to ask questions, to search for answers, but as a masseur there were limitations as to what he could do. But if he were to become a *heilpraktiker*, a naturopath, he would have the same legal status as a medical doctor. He would be free to explore, to develop more systems of his own. Peter Mandel took another jump. He enrolled in the School of the National Association of German Naturopaths in Hanover, some three hours away.

He chose a course that ran from Wednesday evening until noon on Sunday. After working in his own practice from Monday until Wednesday, he would drive to Hanover, attend classes, and be back in Heidelberg late on Sunday afternoon.

'I was hardly ever around. I rarely saw the children, and if I had been Anna – I must say this in her honour – I wouldn't have put up with this situation either,' he said to us. 'I kept saying, "Look, I want to become something and I'm doing this for you and the children." Now I see it wasn't really true. There was this inner drive I couldn't ignore. I *had* to do something nobody else did.'

In naturopathy school, the walls that had hemmed him in came tumbling down. All of a sudden there were new concepts to consider, new tools for his work. He learned about herbal tinctures and homoeopathic injections, about acupuncture and cupping, about ozone and neural therapies. He was like a kid in a toy shop on Christmas Eve.

Give and take had always been one of his greatest joys, and near the end of the course he began inviting his colleagues to the Heidelberg clinic for 'sharings'. They would get together, as many as 40 of an evening, and teach each other their specialities: herbal remedies, massage techniques, ear acupuncture, chiropractic, breathing exercises.

Among the group was one Dr Anton Markgraf, a well-known doctor and the developer of a methodology he called Visual Diagnosis. A master of iridology, the diagnostic system that reads the iris, Markgraf found the method incomplete. He believed that for a comprehensive, foolproof diagnosis, *everything* had to be taken into consideration: eyes, skin, nails, tongue, ears, nose, posture, the shape of the hands, the lines on the face; in other words, the entire man. With Visual Diagnosis he had drawn all these factors together. His premise: if the same indication is visible in all these different areas, then the diagnosis is right.

At first, Mandel told us, he simply couldn't get it. But with his mentor's help and patience, he persevered, wading through hundreds of photographs of eyes and sitting in countless bars and restaurants describing what this facial expression told him, what the curve of this spine or the slope of those shoulders said, what these particular hand gestures revealed. And when the penny finally dropped, when he could finally look and *see* the inner illness mirrored on the surface, 'I felt like Eliza in *My Fair Lady*,' he said. 'It was like a big gnarled knot had opened in my brain.'

Through Markgraf, Mandel learned to look at life spatially; he began to see sickness and health from an holistic point of view. He found he could look into the face of a patient and observe the man's life reflected there – his hopes and fears, his successes and failures – and this whole picture, this overview, began to guide him towards the real culprit, towards the root cause behind the pain.

Now that Peter Mandel could see the wholeness in others, he began to turn this new-found clarity upon himself. He saw he'd been denying an integral part of his own reality for years. It was time to fuse his two worlds into one.

A book gave him the kick he needed. Rudolf Steiner's *Knowledge of the Higher Worlds – How is it Achieved?* Back in 1968 a patient had given it to him, a man whose long-standing pain he'd relieved in a single session. 'You can read it now, but you probably won't understand it,' the client had said. 'But it doesn't matter. Just set it aside and it will call you when it's time.'

'It was really like that,' Mandel said. 'I read 20 pages and put it away. Then, two years later I picked it up again and every word resonated in me.'

Couched in the stilted phraseology of the turn-of-the-century theosophist, Steiner, as a first step, advocates the seeker after higher knowledge to 'steep himself in the lofty thoughts of meditation by men already advanced and inspired by the spirit' – and this was precisely where Mandel began.

He went back to the bookshelf. He read the Tibetans, the Hindus, the Egyptians and the ancient Greeks; he devoured modern mystics like Krishnamurti, Raman Maharshi and Sri Aurobindo; he dabbled in astrology, numerology and the Kabbalah. And the more he read and experimented, the more intuitive flashes came. 'My life changed course, as if what transpired before had been totally unreal,' he said. 'Up to then I had led a normal existence – I worked, I spent time with friends – but I was never very focused. But from this moment on, my life took on a single-minded focus that was totally new to me. And everything began to fall into place.'

The words of Steiner and others, I believe, gave him a context, a framework, and provided a link between what had transpired in his youth and what was happening to him now. He was ripe; it was harvest time, but still he kept missing. When he was treating a patient and an intuition would come, he would follow it – but he would often lose it for the future because he couldn't be bothered to write it down. There was too much else going on.

First of all his mother died, and the experience was shattering. When he speaks of her today, it is still with regret, but with deep gratitude as well. 'I was already a naturopath when she died, but I didn't know much,' he said. 'She was a very strong woman, but her body was destroyed. Today I could have helped her.' And the gratefulness? It was for who she was. 'There was an incredible motherliness about her. It was overwhelming.'

Second, his marriage was collapsing. And then there was work. He was stretching himself farther than any man should. He now had two successful clinics in Heidelberg but was still working over 16 hours a day. And there were more headaches, some of the worst.

Something had to give. In 1973 he decided to pull away. But he did so only partially. He handed the two spine and joint clinics over to his employees and withdrew to the outskirts of Heidelberg where he opened a third practice. He wanted 'a quiet healing clinic for acupuncture and natural medicine', but before he knew it he was booked out again, and back to those killing 16-hour days.

Then, one afternoon, the telephone rang. It was a call to ask if Mandel knew someone who might be interested in buying a clinic from a naturopath's widow, in nearby Bruchsal. He said he couldn't think of anyone offhand.

'That night I decided to buy it myself. I really needed a break, and the Bruchsal clinic sounded ideal: the old man had only a few clients, maybe ten per week, enough to manage, so I planned to treat whosoever came by, but mostly just to sit there and read for the next one or two years.'

Books had always been important – as sources of new and different ideas, as springboards for his own inspiration. While reading, he would jot down insights on little slips of paper, and toss them into a basket he kept at home. And when fragments of diagnostic and healing systems came, in dreams or sudden flashes, he would often find the missing link waiting in his reading basket, scribbled on a scrap of paper.

'So I drove to Bruchsal to check it out,' he said. 'It was dreadful. Everything was old and worn and the whole place was green – the walls, the desks, everything. But I said to myself, "This is exactly what I need: it's so horrible no one will come and I'm sure to have the space I want." '

The first morning he went to the practice, and had just opened his book when the doorbell rang. 'Standing there was an older woman, obviously in pain. I treated her with neural therapy and, immediately, her pain was gone.

'The next morning I went to the practice again, planning to spend another quiet day with my books. I couldn't believe my eyes: there were more than 50 people queuing up the staircase! I quickly ran to the stationery shop next door, bought numbered tickets like they use in government offices, handed them out, rolled up my sleeves and got down to work.'

The woman, it transpires, was the priest's cook. She knew everyone in the parish, and had toured the surrounding villages telling everyone she knew about Mandel. She'd been in pain for such a long time and had been going to doctors and naturopaths for years, and now this new man, this young naturopath, had given her one treatment and her pain was gone.

'Despite myself, I suddenly had another roaring practice again. And this time, all because of the priest's cook and those 50 I treated that first day, a bus now rolled up at my front door at four-thirty every morning, filled with people from the neighbouring towns. I hired some help, a woman who had been a patient, and we worked 18 hours a day. Once, during this period, I even broke my own record. I treated 167 people in a single day.'

He shrugged his shoulders, dropped his agenda and surrendered to the obvious. 'I accepted the fact that life had something else in store for me,' he laughed. 'It must have rescued me from death's door for some purpose. And whatever the reason, it obviously wasn't so I could just sit around and read.

'And from that moment, ideas and intuitions and systems broke over my head like an avalanche.'

4

Energy speaks

We do things when it is our time to do them. They do not occur to us until it is time; they cannot be resisted, once their time has come. It's a question of time, not motive.

BHARATI MUKHERJEE

The Holder of the World

One day in 1972 Peter Mandel took a rare respite from his clients in Heidelberg to visit an exhibition of medical equipment at nearby Baden-Baden. It wasn't that he was looking for anything in particular; he was simply curious to see what was on offer, and looking forward to an excursion, a change of scene. Or so it appeared at the time. But when he set out on his homeward drive that evening, not only had he shelled out 800 marks on a sudden impulse, he now owned a Kirlian camera – with directions in Dutch, a language neither he nor any of his friends could read.

He had no idea how to operate the contraption, and no rational explanation as to why he'd bought it. All he could say was that the advertisement had clinched it. 'Photograph Your Aura!' the exhibit sign had blazoned; 'Take a Picture of Your Soul!' But this ostensibly whimsical purchase, made on this seemingly random outing, was to alter, absolutely, the future direction of his work and the shape of his life. Peter Mandel's moment had come. It was time to start doing that something no one else had ever done before.

When he sold the two Heidelberg practices and shifted to Bruchsal in 1973, leaving everything behind but his clothes and his books and his papers, he brought the Kirlian apparatus with him. And it had been sitting on his desk ever since, eyeing him expectantly. Treating a patient, updating a patient's file or talking on the telephone, the vacant screen's omnipresent gaze seemed to follow him about the room.

And just as the device occupied a corner of his desk, it continued to engage a part of his mind. In the momentary gaps in the stream of patients pouring into his practice, he often found himself contemplating the mystery of the aura, the human energy field.

Books he'd read described the aura as an envelope of iridescence, hidden from normal perception yet girding the body like a mantle of light. Containing all the colours of the rainbow, it was said, by clairvoyants, to emanate outward from the corporal body in layers, or 'energy bodies', of ever-increasing subtlety.

The first subtle body, the etheric, was said to be a holographic energy template governing the physical body's evolution and growth. Second came the astral or emotional body, the vehicle of emotional expression; third, the mental body, the vehicle of intellectual expression; and fourth, the causal or intuitive body, the vehicle of essence. With the final three bodies, specific functions tended to blur into generalities, but psychics and sages basically agreed that these higher-frequency bodies had to do with the most subtle of energies, with the functioning of the human soul.

Mandel was becoming increasingly fascinated by this hidden side of life. More and more, in his work, he was witnessing the effects of the unseen, observing links between physical illness and emotional disturbances. And if, as metaphysics said, the seat of emotion is really situated in the energy field known as the astral body, then, he reasoned, this might very well be where sickness originates. But how to uncover these invisible causes? How to diagnose what he couldn't see?

The aura research of Dr Walter Kilner, a turn-of-the-century English physician, intrigued him. From his experiments, Kilner had arrived at the conclusion that there was a connection between the aura and physical illness. If the aura could ever be photographed effectively, he was convinced, it could help in the diagnosis of illness.

Kilner claimed to have observed the aura through dicyanide-stained glass, describing it as a pulsating cloud some twenty centimetres in depth in which the colours of the spectrum were clearly visible. Over a period, he also observed that certain conditions, including fatigue or mood swings, altered the size of the aura and the colours it emitted. The basic difficulty with the 'Kilner screen' was its reproducibility factor: 50 per cent was insufficient to encourage further scientific interest.

Despite the fact that Mandel didn't know how to operate the camera he'd purchased, he read up on Semjon and Valentina Kirlian, the couple who'd developed the device and given it their name. Working at Russia's Kazakh State University, the husband-and-wife team perfected their photographic technique in the late 1890s, a couple of years after the German physicist Wilhelm Röntgen had discovered X-rays. The Kirlians called their procedure 'electrophotography in a high-frequency field' and claimed it captured, on film, an electrochemical emission or 'radiating luminescence' emitted by all living things. But no one quite knew what these luminous discharges were, or what to do with the photographs.

Still, Mandel was intrigued by the possibilities. If this Kirlian camera of his could really capture the aura on film, as the exhibition sign had promised, what would it tell him? Would the aura really hold clues to the diagnosis of disease, as Kilner had theorized? But even if he succeeded in capturing the aura on film, how would he decipher what he saw?

The drive to get to the root cause behind sickness had become his paramount passion. And accurate diagnosis, he knew, was the very first step. On many occasions he'd found himself facing two patients with precisely the same symptoms only to find that what cured one had no effect on the other. Everybody was different; each man was the sum total of his experiences, his emotions, his lifestyle. Everyone's sickness was uniquely his own.

And Mandel's approach was as uniquely his. He used whatever worked.

One of his prime interests at naturopathy school had been homoeopathy, with its insight that physical symptoms do not exist in isolation, but are a reflection of how people adjust to imbalance in their lives.

He'd found the same attitude in Chinese medicine. To the Chinese, the dynamic balance of yin and yang – of female and male, negative and positive, night and day – is the key to harmony and order. Chinese physicians view the human body as a microcosm of the universe, governed by the same universal energies, by the same cosmic laws.

And more and more, in his practice, Peter Mandel was combining the 'holistic' approach of homoeopathy with the 'energetic' stance of Chinese medicine. At his massage practice in Heidelberg he'd been treating pain by applying pressure on acupuncture points. Now, in Bruchsal, in certain instances, he'd also begun injecting homoeopathic remedies at these same points – and obtaining excellent results.

But he was still dissatisfied with the diagnostic tools he had at his disposal. He was working with Markgraf's Visual Diagnosis method, and with iridology, but he felt the need for a more definitive system, one that revealed more clearly the hidden influences that are an integral component of the total man. His Heidelberg experience in treating spinal complaints had shown him that there is far more to a physical ailment than meets the eye – or is revealed in it. His intuition told him there was something better, something more comprehensive waiting to be discovered. At times he could almost feel it, hovering around.

As week after week went by, and scores of patients came and went, the Kirlian camera continued to track him with its still, expressionless stare. Then, one day, his brother came for a visit. 'You have technical flair, Eberhard,' he said. 'Why don't you take this thing home with you and see if you can figure it out?'

Eberhard went back to Pforzheim with the Kirlian machine under his arm. And for a while Mandel simply forgot about it. As usual, there was too much else going on. That bus from the surrounding villages was still pulling up in front of his practice before dawn, and then, promptly at eight, his local Bruchsal patients began trooping through the door.

The toll was beginning to tell, and one morning he told the people from the bus he simply couldn't go on like this any longer. 'I have to sleep once in a while too,' he said, 'so instead of you coming here all the time I'll come to you once a week. It'll be cheaper for you and, besides, this is killing me.' He opened a second practice in nearby Bad Kreuznach. And he hired more help.

Now that he had the occasional free moment, he decided to go to Pforzheim. There'd been no news about the Kirlian camera and he was curious to see if his brother had been able to get it to work. He also had a severe case of enteritis and badly needed a break.

Despite the Dutch directions the Kirlian camera was ready to go. Eberhard placed a sheet of black and white photographic paper on the exposure plate and asked, 'So, what do we photograph?'

Mandel placed his right hand on the paper. 'This,' he replied.

The results, when the photo had been developed, utterly astounded him. The tip of each finger was characterized by a very long and brilliant luminescence, except for the index and little fingers, which showed virtually no emission at all. And in his mind, like tumblers in a padlock, a sequence of conclusions began to click into place.

When Mandel first laid his hand on the Kirlian screen his guts had been in a painful knot from the enteritis. And he had a suspicion it was this intestinal condition he was seeing reflected on the photo! In Chinese acupuncture, the meridian for the large intestine begins in the index finger, and the meridian for the small intestine in the little finger – and these were the two fingers which showed a total lack of radiation!

'Let's see what happens if I bring my symptoms under control,' he said to his brother, inserting a gold acupuncture needle into a point at the base of his right thumb, on the large-intestine meridian. As soon as he felt better, they took another picture. In this second photograph, the radiation from every finger was of equal strength and luminescence.

After a couple of hours, when the cramps and the diarrhoea returned, they tried again. And there, on the third photograph, was the result he expected: once again there was no emission from the index and little fingers.

'I was unbelievably excited,' he said. 'It was as if I had stumbled on to a treasure chest and, finally managing to pry it open, found it overflowing with infinite ideas and possibilities.' He sensed he was on to something spectacular. This could well be a new and important diagnostic tool – and he couldn't wait to get back to his practice to try it out with his patients.

But, typically, he'd already seen how the apparatus could be improved. 'You know,' he said to his brother, 'I'm pretty sure there is something to this Kirlian thing, but this machine is so small it's going to be awkward to work with. Do you think you could develop something bigger?'

'Easily,' Eberhard replied. 'All I need to do is use a larger glass plate. The electronics will be exactly the same.'

But what about a more total view? Mandel wondered, remembering that both polarity *and* laterality are important factors in the diagnostic approach of Chinese medicine. 'I can't see how a photograph of one hand is going to give me a whole picture of a patient's condition,' he mused. 'If illness is imbalance, like the Chinese say, I've got to be able to look at right and left, at upper and lower. I think we should photograph both hands, and the feet as well.'

'No problem,' his brother answered. 'We use two exposure plates, one above and one below. First we photograph the hands, and then move the photographic paper down, lay it on the second plate and take a picture of the feet.'

From the moment he installed the modified Kirlian camera in Bruchsal, every patient who walked into the practice had a photo taken of fingers and toes. And slowly, slowly, the coronas exploding on to the photographic paper began to reveal their secrets.

One of Mandel's first successes with the Kirlian involved a young mother suffering from puerperal or 'childbed' psychosis. She was completely distracted when she arrived at the clinic. Something was very wrong: she couldn't stand her newborn child, and the doctors had taken it away for fear she would harm it. She'd been everywhere, tried everything. Did he think he could help?

She came to him during the time he was trying to establish a topography, puzzling over which finger or toe related to which particular organ or body system. At the bottom of the emanation from the woman's left index finger, he observed a dark, congested cluster of points. This emission differed dramatically from those of the other fingers, and he took it as a sign that something was very definitely out of kilter.

Remembering the abnormality in the emission from his own index finger when he'd taken the first Kirlian picture at his brother's, and recalling how he'd been able to link it to his enteritis, he calculated that the top half of the fingertip might well represent the upper section of the torso, and the bottom half, the lower part of the body. Something, he reasoned, must be going on in the woman's abdomen. 'Go to your gynaecologist and have yourself checked,' he advised.

The gynaecologist, the young mother reported afterwards, was reluctant to examine her at first, maintaining that nothing was physically wrong. But she insisted. And Mandel had been right. Something *was* amiss in her abdomen: a piece of the placenta was still lodged inside her womb. The moment it was removed, the puerperal psychosis disappeared.

Mandel was tremendously encouraged by this news. And his conviction grew that he was, indeed, on the threshold of developing a new diagnostic tool.

Precisely what it was he was actually capturing on photographic paper, however, he couldn't say for sure. He sensed it wasn't the aura Kilner had identified through dicyanide-stained glass. Whatever he was photographing wasn't simply a sheath surrounding the body, it was a force coursing *through* it, bursting from its extremities in tiny invisible sparks. All he knew for certain was that he was dealing with energy.[1]

Still, his mind wanted an explanation. Initially, because the Chinese acupuncture meridians terminate at the fingers and toes, he'd thought the emissions might be connected to the *ch'i*, to the life-force flowing through the meridians. The current of *ch'i* is another of the body's circadian rhythms, and it has been shown that the life-energy circulates through each meridian 25 times every day or night.[2] At first he thought the radiation emission was dependent on this ebb and flow of energy, on the tide of yin and yang, but in that first year of experimentation, from correlating the Kirlians of his patients with their symptoms, he reached the conclusion that the emissions were showing him something else.

He also began to explore other energy networks. Among these were new meridians discovered by the developer of electroacupuncture,[3] the German physician, Dr Reinhard Voll. For example, one of Voll's new pathways was a 'nerve degeneration' channel running alongside the Chinese large-intestine meridian beginning at the tip of the index finger. To Mandel, the name itself offered an important clue. If a nerve is degenerating, he reasoned, then it must also be degenerating at its source; in other words, at the spine. In the Kirlian picture, he therefore concluded, the condition of the spine, as well as the large intestine, must be revealed in the radiation emitted by the index finger.

And so, for the next several weeks, everyone who came to the practice with a spinal complaint underwent intensive scrutiny, as well as photographing before and after treatment. Mandel would ask, 'Where is your pain?', then pinpoint precisely where the symptom appeared on the Kirlian photo. And whatever the ailment, he followed the same procedure, whether it was with joints or muscles, stomach or intestines, liver or lungs.

And somewhere along the line he stopped listening to the questions of his mind – Were the emissions part of the aura? Or the *ch'i*? Or Voll's bio-electric network? – and just accepted the fact that, once again, he'd chanced upon something new, that once more he was doing something no one else had done. The Kirlian pictures were giving him clues to help heal his patient's aches and pains and illnesses, and that was enough. 'I'm obviously dealing with a closed energy field,' he said to himself. And let it go at that. Like Shakespeare – 'A rose by any other name would smell as sweet' – Mandel had never attached much importance to labels anyway.

An extremely important plus during these early days of attempting to decipher the Kirlians was the possibility of weighing his own conclusions against concrete medical evidence. 'People came to us from doctors and clinics, and they always brought their medical reports with them,' he said. 'And I often sat long into the night with a stack of Kirlian photos alongside a heap of medical reports, relating one to the other.'

As he pored over the Kirlians, checking his findings again and again against his patients' histories and their responses to treatment, he grew more and more convinced that not only was he witnessing manifest energy, he was also dealing with coded information that needed to be deciphered before it could be understood.

He studied a staggering number of Kirlian photos – 800,000 in all – comparing them with clinical laboratory reports and with his own observations before, at the end of 1974, he established the hypothesis that was to form the foundation of the diagnostic system he named Energy Emission Analysis (EEA).

In *Energy Emission Analysis: New Application of Kirlian Photography for Holistic Health*, published in 1983, he wrote: 'Through the use of the high-frequency apparatus, it was obvious that we were dealing with energy, and I therefore ascribed all cellular processes that take place within individuals as belonging to this energy.

'It later became evident that our presumptions were correct . . . Through our observations, it became evident that long before symptoms manifest, bodily changes, disease or illness are energetically existent and through our photographic technique would reveal themselves.'

It was apparent that the Kirlian photos were providing an opportunity to 'see' pathological processes taking place. Through the EEA pictures, Mandel found he could detect potential diseases, with our without symptoms, which had been developing for years or were present in their prodromal or 'approaching' states. And he suddenly found he no longer needed to compare his findings with medical and laboratory reports.

'I said if what I have accomplished up to now is correct, then the reverse must also be true: if someone comes to me I must be able to tell him what is going on with him from what I see in the photos. I found I was able to tell someone that he has this specific symptom because this particular thing is going on with him. We were taking the step back to the root-cause of the disease.'

Describing the process of sickness as 'a causal chain of events', he added: 'The most important goal of analysis is to discover, if possible, the causal relationships in order to reach the source of the problem. With the energy pictures, the most significant aspect of their analysis potential is the possibility of detecting the first functional changes in individuals, and doing so early enough to eliminate any resulting alterations or imbalances in organs or physical processes.

'And this was completely new,' he told Verena and me. 'Diagnoses like this were never included in traditional allopathic medical reports.'

It is in terms of preventative medicine, however, that the implications of Mandel's Kirlian diagnostic system were, and are, truly enormous.

His EEA, Mandel realized even then, offers a possibility for early diagnosis and follow-up therapeutic intervention, thereby preventing transition to a more advanced state of an illness. 'Clinically manifested disease is topographically depicted on organ sectors in EEA pictures, and the structure of the phenomena offers exact information concerning the developmental stage of the disease,' he said. 'It is obviously more beneficial to regulate the disease in an asymptomatic stage, before symptoms appear, than to wait for the process to manifest itself clinically.

'Another aim is to prevent "negative" developmental processes from appearing by use of therapeutic intervention *before* clinically manifested states appear. Medical ethics dictates the doctrine of prevention of disease. The analytic possibilities of EEA and subsequent therapeutic intervention allow these ethical demands to be fulfilled.'

By the time he published his book in 1983, he had also established a topography (figure 1).

For the energy radiations from the fingers, he concluded that the condition of the heart and the small intestine was reflected in the emission from the little finger; the psyche and the endocrine or hormonal system in the corona emanating from the ring finger; circulation and sex energy, as well as vascular degeneration, from the middle finger; nerve degeneration and the large intestine from the index finger; lungs and the lymph system from the thumb.

The big toe, he had deduced, revealed the condition of the spleen, pancreas and the liver; the next toe, the stomach and degeneration of the joints; the middle toe, degeneration of the skin and connective

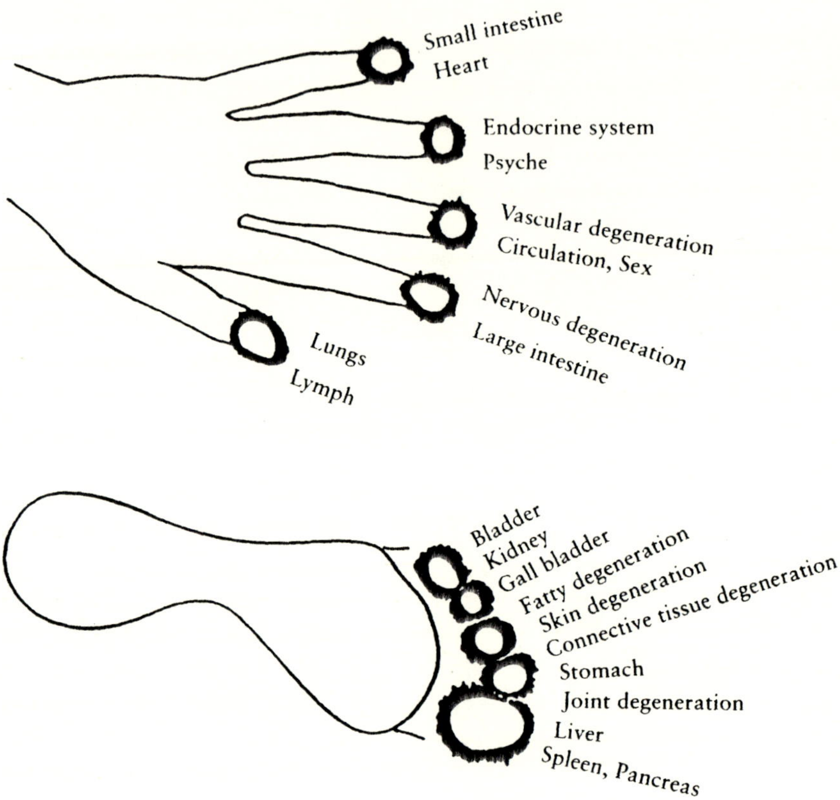

Figure 1 EEA topography established by Peter Mandel

tissue; the next, the gall bladder and the degeneration of the body's fatty tissues; and the little toe, the kidneys and the bladder.

Topography complete, Mandel started sharing his discovery – through seminars for doctors and therapists in Germany. And working with VEGA, a medical device manufacturer in the Black Forest, he developed a Kirlian machine which he offered for sale. And so the cycle of events begun that day in Baden-Baden came full circle. 'I sometimes find it really unbelievable how an apparent coincidence, coupled with the power of thought and intuition, was able to open up a whole new dimension in such a seemingly well-known and well-researched field as medical diagnostics,' he said. 'It still amazes me at times.'

Tracking the root cause of disease

For an independent and practical illustration of EEA at work, I decided to take a chronological jump to the present and consult a practising physician who uses Mandel's Kirlian system for diagnosis and Colourpuncture as her primary therapeutic tool.

At the time we spoke, Dr Jaldhara Kristen, a 1986 graduate of the School of Medicine at Switzerland's University of Basel, operated a busy practice in downtown Zurich. She'd been working with Mandel's system for over five years, and also taught it: through regular weekend Colourpuncture and Kirlian training events in the Zurich area, as well as workshops in Germany for the Thalamus Heilpraktikerschulen, a Cologne-based college of naturopathy.

Mandel's blending of a scientific Western approach with the Eastern understanding of the unity of spirit-soul-body was what initially attracted her to his work, she said. His approach resonated with a direction she knew, intuitively, was also the way she wanted to go.

Dissatisfaction with the conventional medical approach to healing began in medical school, with the realization, as she put it, that 'allopathy starts too late'.

The child of doctors, medicine was in her blood. 'I always had this fascination with the mystery of the body, with how life works,' she said, 'and the first few years at university were thrilling.' But the moment the curriculum expanded to include the study of disease, her enchantment turned to disillusion. 'We know so little about where a disease comes from, or why someone gets sick. I wanted to know *why* one woman gets a tumour in the bladder and another woman gets one in the breast, but there were no answers. Medical science only starts to work when someone is already ill. This didn't satisfy me. It's too late.'

Nonetheless, she finished medical school and, after three years internship in gynaecology, obstetrics and internal medicine in Swiss hospitals, accepted her first doctoring job – as a locum in an Alpine village for a holidaying physician. It was to be the turning point.

'There I was, sitting behind a desk, wearing a white coat and a name tag, and people came to me in total trust. "I'm not feeling well; something is wrong," they would tell me. I would do all the lab tests and in many, many cases nothing would show up. I would have to go back to them and say, "The lab tests are all negative, so just relax."

'But I knew they were right, that something *was* wrong. And I didn't know what to do. The tools I had at my disposal simply weren't substantial enough.'

Pain is what brings most people to a doctor, and her first step, like Mandel's, is to provide whatever relief she can. At the same time, she tries to help her patients see that pain is not just an unpleasantness to be rid of, but a clear message from the body that some aspect of their being – physical, emotional and/or spiritual – is crying out for attention.

Her second effort is to make them realize that neither she nor any doctor can remove the *cause* of their pain. This is the responsibility of the patient alone.

'In a Colourpuncture session we look at where the pain is, at what comes up, at what the pain is saying, and I help translate the language of the body so that we can work our way back to the root cause of the pain, at whichever level of being it originates. And pain is always related to areas of our lives we really don't want to look into.

'When I apply colour – using whatever therapy is indicated by the clues we uncover – I tell my patients to close their eyes, look in, and feel whatever is there. The colour sets a certain machinery in motion, and by turning their vision inward and looking into those dark, hidden corners, often for the first time, people start to take responsibility for their own sickness. Then their lives begin to change, and their aches and pains begin to disappear.'

Although the evolution of Colourpuncture and its treatments will be examined in later chapters, it will be helpful, prior to presenting Dr Kristen's sample EEA readings, to provide a brief overview of one of the basic concepts Colourpuncture employs to guide the therapist towards the root cause behind an illness: the five interrelated organ circuits, or 'function circles', defined by the Munich ear, nose and throat specialist, Dr Jochen Gleditsch.

Gleditsch's five function circles have deep roots in medical history: they are found in Chinese medicine as water, wood, metal, earth and fire (the elements of which all living things are comprised), and as the five *entias* of Paracelsus, the 16th-century Swiss physician and alchemist who, way back then, was already promoting a holistic medical vision.

Many complex relationships are at play in these five organ circuits. On a physical level, they govern not only the organ groupings from which they derive their names, but various other body systems and functions as well. And these body parts and processes are also deeply connected to, and affected by, specific mental, emotional and spiritual states.

Each organ circuit also mirrors the polarity inherent in life itself, and is characterized by negative and positive emotions, like the two sides of a coin. In addition, each circuit is related to an external sensory organ – in the two-fold sense of inner and outer perception.

'Any disturbances in these organ circuits affect even the smallest areas of our lives, and are shared with the whole system via cellular bio-communication,' Mandel explained. 'This means that an external manifestation, physical or emotional, is an indication that the related organ circuit requires therapeutic attention.

'The EEA phenomena always show the complete picture. All the interrelations between all five circuits are evident, so a predominance of any one of them is easily recognizable. Then, with great certainty, the therapist can determine which particular organ circuit needs treatment.' And treatment, in Colourpuncture, means uncovering the hidden source of illness and bringing it to conscious awareness, where it can be faced and resolved.

Gleditsch's first organ circuit is the kidney/bladder function circle. Physically, this function circle governs the kidneys, bladder, lymph system, genitals, ovaries and the bones, and is also related to the knees. The ear is its external organ, both in terms of hearing the sounds of the outer world as well as listening to the still small voice within. Emotionally, the positive side of the organ circuit is trust; the negative, fear. The kidney/bladder circuit corresponds to the Chinese element water, and to the *ens naturale* of Paracelsus.

Dr Kristen asserts that the root cause of a physical disorder can invariably be found in one of the deeper levels of life; in other words, in some mental, emotional or spiritual disturbance. 'It doesn't matter if the kidney/bladder function circle expresses in the knee or in the ear, as a bladder or a vaginal infection, the issue is always the same,' she stated. 'And sometimes if you treat one symptom – like prescribing antibiotics for a bladder infection – the next thing which happens is that the patient gets an infection in the ear. Because the basic problem hasn't been looked at. And that is fear, in some kind of disguise.'

The second organ circuit is liver/gall-bladder. This is the *ens astrale* of Paracelsus, and the wood element of the Chinese. On the one hand, it is about expressing emotions (anger, first of all); on the other, it's about flexibility and tolerance. The sensory organ is the eye; the physical aspects: the liver, gall-bladder, muscles and sinews.

The third organ circuit, lung/large intestine, governs the lungs, the large intestine, the skin, the hair and the body's immune system, and is linked to the Chinese element, metal, and to Paracelsus's *ens spirituale*. The emotions: on the one hand, melancholy; on the other, intuition and letting go. The sensory organ is the nose, both in its outer olfactory application as well as the inner sense of 'smelling' trouble or danger.

The fourth function circle is spleen-pancreas/stomach. It relates to the *ens veneni* of Paracelsus and the Chinese element, earth. The stomach, spleen, pancreas, joints, throat and sinuses belong to this circuit, and the sensory key is the mouth and lips. One side of the emotional coin is stress, the other is meditation.

'This function circle has a lot to do with the mind,' Dr Kristen explained. 'Somehow, under stress, all the energy goes into thinking, into worrying, and it's usually the stomach that's affected. A disturbance like hyperacidity can develop, for example, and cause ulcers. That's why the opposite aspect of this function circle is meditation. The only way out of this trap of tension is to relax and step out of the mind.'

The final function circle, heart/small intestine, holds a special place within the five circuits. It represents the spiritual aspect of our beings, and corresponds to joy, enthusiasm, sympathy and the warmth of the spiritual heart. The tongue as the organ of speech is one functional key; the blood and its circulatory system, another. In Chinese medicine, this organ circuit is represented by fire. It is the *ens dei* of Paracelsus.

'The first four function circles, in a way, protect the fifth, the heart, so it doesn't get damaged,' Dr Kristen said. 'But if we don't resolve the issues of the four function circles; if we don't look at our stuff, the heart is going to be affected, weakened. It's like a bowl into which liquid is poured and poured until it eventually spills over.'

She cites standard medical evidence to support her statement: 'If the kidneys are not filtering properly, and leaving too much water volume in the blood system, this will create high blood pressure, which is eventually going to be a heart problem. Liver congestion, if untreated, will also hurt the heart, as will lung problems like emphysema. And the stomach's response to stress is always acidity. The inner lining of the heart is very sensitive to acidity, and some doctors believe heart attacks are the end result of excess acidity.'

In one of the case histories she selected to illustrate Kirlian photography as a diagnostic tool, this is precisely what is happening.

Simone came to Dr Kristen not about her heart, but about severe stomach cramps. A single mother, 40 years of age, she is a classical musician with trouble finding regular work. And financially, as well as emotionally, she alone is responsible for her six-year-old daughter. By nature a caring and conscientious mother, she wants to give her child the best she possibly can. But it's hard. She's often not home when the girl returns from school, and when she is, and her daughter needs her attention, the cramps become so bad she has to lie down. And then she feels guilty. 'I'm trapped in this vicious circle,' she told Dr Kristen. 'I'm burning up all my energy and nothing productive is coming out of it.'

When she began to examine Simone's Kirlian photo (figure 2), Dr Kristen's attention was first drawn to the fact that all of the fingers were characterized by a very small white field surrounded by a thick rim of blackness.

Indicating this area on the photo, she asked me to imagine a tiny human being standing in this white field. And since the white field represents the space one allows oneself, it was apparent, even to me,

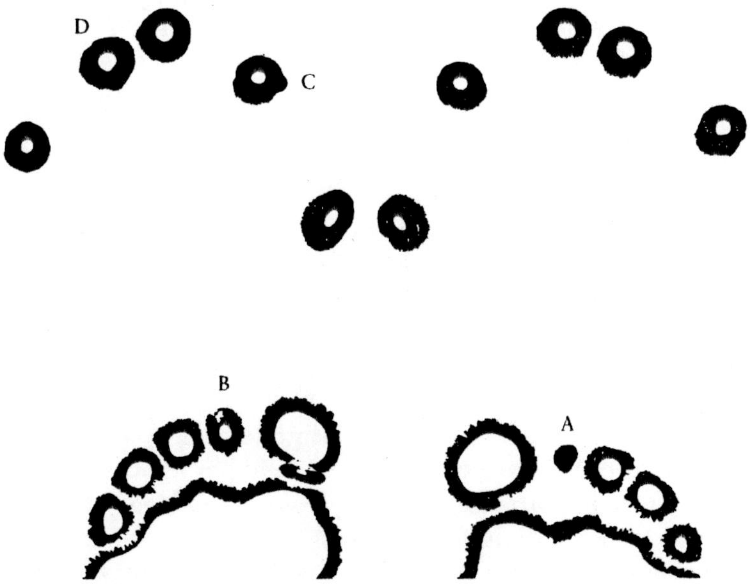

Figure 2 Kirlian photo of Simone examined by Dr Kristen

that Simone was extremely hemmed in, and that she didn't have much room in her life for herself. In addition, the top of each white field was somewhat flat – an indication, Dr Kristen explained, of heavy pressure on the head and a predominance of mental activity.

'There is also a rigidity in the energetic system,' she said, pointing to the thick layer of radiation around the fingers. 'This means there is a space of protection around this woman, and it's getting so thick it protects very well, but standing inside this dense wall, nothing can really reach her. She's in a very stuck situation.'

Her next conclusion had to do with the predominance of 'hairs' extending downwards, like tiny roots, from the bottom of most finger emissions. 'Peter Mandel always says these long radiations show an attempt to create security in one's life, and whereas the being actually yearns to grow in all directions, this person is only growing in a very material way. In Simone's picture, this appraisal is reinforced by the downward mental pressure revealed in the upper parts of the fingers.'

Moving to the feet, Dr Kristen indicated the complete absence of a white field on the second toe of the right foot (A) and the cramped field on the left (B). This toe is related to the stomach, where Simone complained of cramps.

The spleen-pancreas/stomach function circle, as she'd explained earlier, has a great deal to do with the mind. 'All Simone's energy is used up in "Shall I do this?" or "Shall I do that?",' Dr Kristen continued. 'And when I asked her about it, she said this is precisely what happens, that at night she is so busy worrying about what to do she has great difficulty sleeping.'

The Kirlian also revealed problems with the colon, indicated by a dark 'blob' on the index finger (C) – and a clump such as this is an indication of a developing difficulty in an organ sector. There was also a second blob, a double one, on the left ring finger (D). 'This finger carries the hormonal glands, and the pituitary and the hypothalamus, the so-called "masters of the hormonal glands", are located at the top of the fingers. Treating these would help resolve part of her situation.'

To Dr Kristen, relaxation was Simone's key, and she used Colourpuncture systems designed to expand her inner space and to relax the stomach area. She also decided to treat the spleen-pancreas/stomach function circle.

Next she took a control picture (figure 3) to analyse the effectiveness of the treatment and evaluate how to proceed further.

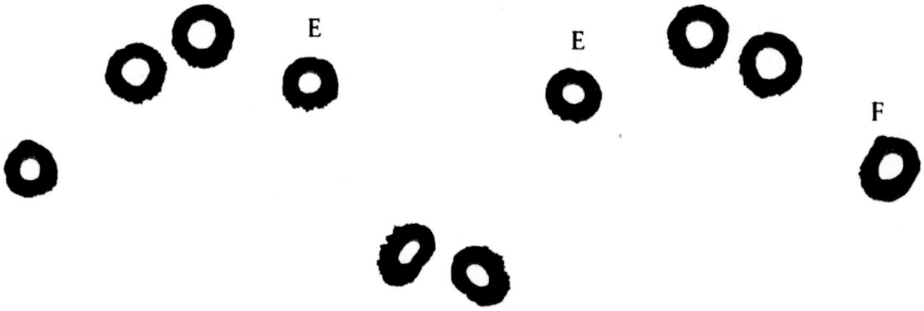

Figure 3 Control picture of Simone

In the follow-up Kirlian, the expansion is evident in the enlarged finger fields, the protecting walls are thinner and finer details are more evident, as if an 'energy veil' had been lifted. 'For me, this was a sign that a relaxation, an opening had occurred, and I was much more able to see *behind* what was going on.'

What she saw was that the index fingers (E) had remained cramped. The index fingers reveal the connection between two parts of the brain, between the medulla oblongata, the seat of involuntary functions like the heartbeat, and the thalamus, the door to consciousness. In Simone's case, this connection between the medulla and the thalamus needed attention. Things were not getting through.

'The situation in the index finger shows she needs to become more aware of things; it's a hint that she now has to adjust to a new reality. And in her next session I would include a treatment to relax this connection, to help her bring more aspects of her life to consciousness.

'After the first treatment Simone told me how much better she felt, how much more relaxed, and this tells me, as we continue to work together, that this woman is going to be able to let go of the rigid structure in which she's been confined.'

Dr Kristen also said there was one other significant phenomenon that had surfaced in the second picture, and that was a dark blob (F) on the little finger of the right hand, the area of the entrance to the heart. 'This tells me these issues in her life have already touched her heart, perhaps not physically but certainly energetically,' she said. 'Unless this is dealt with, she may end up with some kind of heart problem. This is a sign we will have to look at her blood pressure, because highs and lows in blood pressure are often aggravated by stress.'

The second illustration Dr Kristen chose was Frank, 46, a homoeopath who came to her complaining of extreme tension in the right side of his neck. But when Dr Kristen scanned his Kirlian picture (figure 4) she realized the neck was just the tip of the iceberg.

First of all, his feet hardly showed up at all, revealing a strong imbalance in the energy flow between the upper and lower parts of his body. The cut-off point is always the solar plexus, and when she asked if he felt anything there, he said yes, he sometimes feels a pressure in that area and often has the sensation that he doesn't have enough space to breathe.

Since the feet contain the abdominal organs, and the lack of energy was obvious, she also concluded he was running on reserve. Frank confirmed her diagnosis, saying even if he sleeps eight or ten

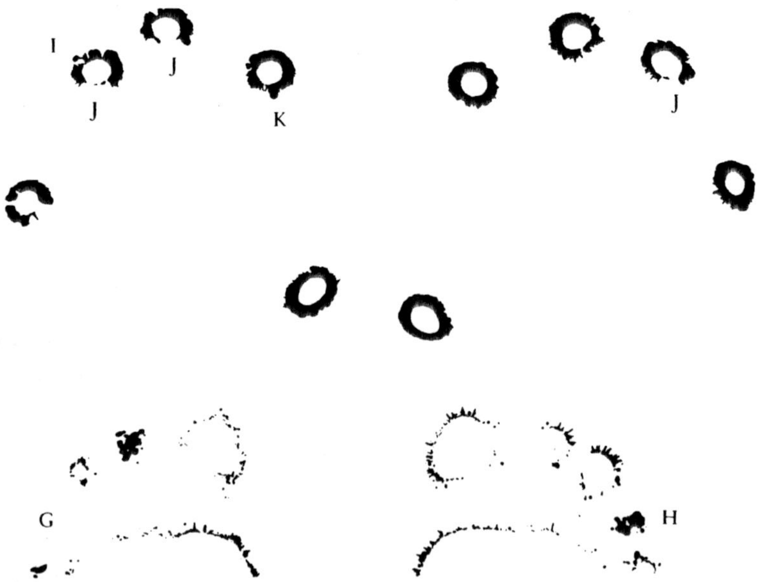

Figure 4 Kirlian photo of Frank, examined by Dr Kristen

hours a night he's always exhausted in the morning. 'Really faint feet in a Kirlian picture show that a patient can't manage to recharge his batteries, so there's a sluggishness in the whole metabolism,' Dr Kristen said.

Looking more closely, she noticed that one left toe was missing completely (G) and the corresponding toe on the right foot was extremely contracted (H) – and this is the toe which relates to the gall-bladder. 'In Chinese medicine the gall-bladder is where emotions are stored,' she explained. 'The gall-bladder is the sister of the liver: the liver gives life-energy to the emotions, but if this energy is not used the emotions are stored in the gall-bladder. If someone is stockpiling emotions, and never expressing them, more and more storage space is needed until, at some point, these stored emotions solidify into gallstones. And the emotions we're talking about here are the strong, loud ones, like frustration, anger and hate.'

She asked what was going on in his life. Frank, it transpired, was in a relationship where the woman was seeing other men, and he couldn't handle it. The woman simply said, 'That's *your* stuff; *you* deal with it.' There was no space to express his anger. He was sitting on a volcano.

'I also noticed a fly-away point on the left ring finger (I),' Dr Kristen continued. 'This is the location of the thyroid gland, and a point flying away on the outer edge of an emission is a reactive sign.' After asking about physical thyroid symptoms like problems with his weight, and receiving a negative response, she touched on the emotional aspect of the thyroid, the connection to one's father. From what he'd already told her, and from what she saw in the Kirlian, it was not only apparent that Frank was suppressing his anger, it was also obvious that he was sitting on his male energy. 'I didn't say this to him, but I wanted to see if there was a pattern here.'

His father, he told her, was a very soft and heartful man, and as a child he'd adored him. His mother, on the other hand, he didn't like. A tough businesswoman, she organized the lives of her husband and children to fit into her schedule. 'I didn't say this to him either, but it was apparent that his male role model didn't exhibit too much male energy, in terms of stamina or standing up for himself. And he's followed his father's model by picking a similar kind of woman for himself.'

Another outstanding feature of his Kirlian were the big holes at the bottom of three fingers (J), all kidney/bladder areas. 'This is the whole sexual area, the prostate, the testes, and indicates an insufficiency,' she said. 'This was another confirmation that he is cutting off his sexuality.'

Dr Kristen also noticed yet another point in flight on the left index finger (K), in a position relating to the coccyx. 'He said there were no physical problems, no pain, no haemorrhoids, no accidental fall, so I deduced another level must be involved. In Mandel's methodology, the coccyx relates to the thalamus, to bringing issues to consciousness, and this sign in the picture told me it's very important for him to take a long, hard look at what's happening in his life, even though he doesn't want to. Again, I didn't say this to him, and for a particular reason.

'To me, just talking to a patient about his or her psychological patterns solves nothing. The realizations that people need to address their problems must come from inside them, and Colourpuncture facilitates this process.

'This is why I only asked Frank about his body symptoms. I see he cuts himself off from his life-energy, and I want to be able to dissolve this blockage so that he can stand on his own two feet, feel himself more, get in touch with his anger and frustration and resolve the mess he's put himself in. And that is what we started to do in this first session.'

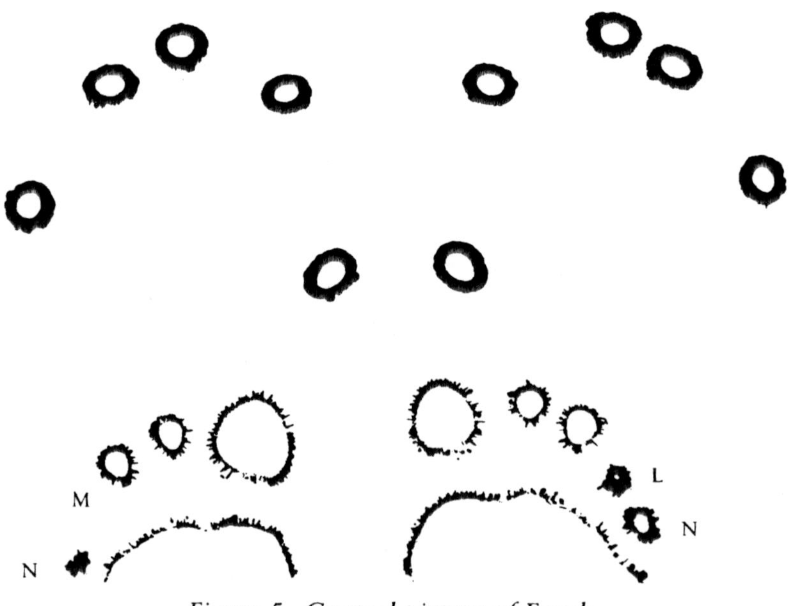

Figure 5 Control picture of Frank

Dr Kristen used Colourpuncture treatments to balance left and right, to open up the solar plexus area, to stimulate lymph flow, and a detoxing procedure to help eliminate the body toxins accumulated as a result of his general immobility.

In his control picture (figure 5) the balance between left and right, upper and lower, is more obviously harmonious. The new strength in the feet also indicates that he's no longer simply running on reserve, but that his life-juices are beginning to flow.

The gall-bladder issue is still in evidence. But it has improved. There is now a small white field on the right (L), but on the left (M) the toe is still missing. 'This is a much better starting point for him to begin to acknowledge his anger,' Dr Kristen noted.

The little toes (N) showed up in the original picture as well, but she let them go by – because these toes relate to the kidney/bladder function circle, and the issue is fear. 'The anger is in front and the fear is behind it,' she said. 'And before he can handle the fear, he first has to deal with the anger.'

And she's confident that this will happen when the time is right. The disappearance of the fly-away, thalamus point on the left index finger (K in figure 4) is an indication that inside Frank some realizations have begun to dawn. 'It doesn't need to be in words. This is something that happens silently inside.'

And his neck? 'We never even talked about it,' she laughed, 'but when he left he said it was better.'

And subsequent treatments? In the next session she'll focus on creating space for him to express his emotions, with Colourpuncture treatments for the limbic system. 'The limbic system is like a switchboard for filtering emotions,' she explained. 'It accepts emotions that are known and rejects those that are not. From my observation, I don't believe he feels his anger yet, or even realizes it's there. And for sure he's not aware of the fear behind it. Treating the limbic system will begin to open things up so the hidden issues begin to surface, but slowly, so he can deal with it.

'This, for me, is the great thing about Colourpuncture. There's no need to break through any mental barrier. By treating with colour, the correct, healing information is introduced energetically, and the understanding the patient needs to resolve his problems arises on its own.'

5

The holistic miracle

We are spiritual beings having a physical experience.
DEEPAK CHOPRA MD

An awakening is a shift in consciousness. Suddenly an inner light goes on, there's instant clarity, and one is never the same again. Like the day I realized I wasn't the centre of the universe.

I was a fat kid, compensating for an absent mother by a relationship with the fridge. As the rolls of blubber grew and my self-esteem dwindled, even walking down the street became a torture. Everyone was talking about me, laughing at me behind my back. 'His mother died because of him,' I was sure they were saying. 'And no wonder! Look how fat and repulsive he is!'

On the way home from school one afternoon – I must have been six or seven – a couple came towards me on the footpath, engaged in conversation. Of course they were talking about me! Wasn't I everyone's primary concern? But as they passed I saw they paid me no attention whatsoever. They were preoccupied with themselves, just as I was with me.

A light flashed on in my head – I recall the sensation exactly – and I understood that each of us is the centre of his or her own universe, and that there are as many universes as there are individuals. And then a burden dropped from my chubby little shoulders and, all at once, I felt wonderfully free.

On another level, my perspective remained egocentric. I continued to think that the mixture of material and mental was the sum total of *me*.

That illusion shattered on the New York State Thruway, the night life demolished my sense of self along with my car. Through my own experience, I learned that I am a great deal more than I'd thought I was. Beyond the finite mind lies an infinity of silence. And the very stuff of being is the energy of light.

Many of us taste this greater totality from time to time. Playing a piano or painting a picture, sewing a dress or tending the garden, there's a sudden realization that, for a while, no 'I', no doer has been present, just a silent creativity, manifesting invisibly, like a gentle breeze through a hollow bamboo. Or, sitting in meditation, there's a blurring of boundaries, a sense of dissolving, a whiff of the oneness of which we all are waves.

Egocentric attitudes, however, still hold the majority of people captive. And to be trapped in a false standpoint is limiting, stunting, a hindrance to living the richness that is our birthright.

Language is one of the great limiters. The words we use are ancient in origin, and so, in many cases, is the information they convey. Consider the word 'sunset'. Viewed from a world that was thought to be flat, of course the sun set. But it only *appears* that way. The reality, it was discovered later, is that our planet spins on its axis, circling the sun.

We live in a world of illusions; freedom lies in transcending them. And so I continue to use the word 'sunset' – it's familiar, utilitarian – but every time I remind myself: remember what is really going on. Actually, remembering adds to the mystery; it enhances my awe.

The human mind, with its self-serving righteousness and prejudices, can be another great limiter. And nowhere is this more evident than in mainstream medical science. If something can't be weighed or measured or analyzed, if it can't be explained to the mind's satisfaction, it's dismissed or ignored.

Fortunately, in the quest to alleviate man's suffering, there is another breed of scientist at work. These men and women are masters of their minds, not slaves to the mind's machinations and misconceptions. They have learned to use this mind, this biocomputer, as a tool to plumb the depths of illusion and ferret out the truth.

They have also learned to transcend the limits of language, to create new concepts, to bring new meanings to old words. Through metaphor and analogy, through symbols and clues, they are able to harness their insights and communicate mystery in the language of the mind.

The term 'Esogetics' is such an endeavour. Peter Mandel created it to convey, in a single word, his 'thought-model', his integrated vision for a whole and healthy man or woman.

'Esogetics,' he explained in the preface to his book of the same name, 'is the merger of the esoteric wisdom of life with the energetic principles of life's processes.'

The model gave him a context, a conceptual tool, 'a common roof', as he phrased it, to encompass the methods he'd developed to date. At the same time, he found that once he had given his thought-model form, it also acted as an catalyst for fresh ideas. 'In recognizing and treating illness, many new perspectives arose out of this synthesis,' he wrote. 'I also saw that I was better and better able to show ill people the meaning of their sicknesses, and to encourage them to look into that which is making them unwell.'

The only demand Esogetics makes of us is that we acknowledge one simple truth we innately know – that there's more to life than greets the eye. 'Once one accepts dimensions that are as yet unproven, Esogetics is totally logical and amazingly simple,' he stated. 'That's why I have such a strong inner urge to share it with as many people as possible.'

Sharing Mandel's Esogetic Model (and the steps that led to its formulation) is also this chapter's intent – and the aim of these introductory remarks is to remind the reader that not only do 'dimensions that are as yet unproven' indeed exist, they make their presence felt in countless ways, each and every day.

In addition, I wish to invoke a broader perspective on who we really are. We are not the Newtonian mechanisms of Western medicine, machines that malfunction from time to time; we are dynamic Einsteinian systems – a multidimensional cohesion of energy fields, interdependent and interfacing, integrated into a miraculous, individual oneness reflecting the greater whole. And everything, from conscious thought to cellular process, is an electromagnetic oscillation, a degree of frequency vibration, a biomanifestation of the one primal energy, the energy of light.

Esogetic medicine is a medicine of energy; it's vibrational healing, 21st-century style. And as such, it merits a scrutiny that's also mature, untainted by outdated ideas and egocentric attitudes. Esogetic medicine deserves the sort of consideration author Ken Wilber calls 'a curious blend of deduction, induction, intuition, sensation and insight'. It's a challenge to trust our intrinsic knowing, the 'still, small voice' that resides within.

Between 1973, when he settled in Bruchsal, and 1976, when he first shared his Esogetic vision in public lectures and seminars, Peter Mandel's 'still small voice' was a loudspeaker, broadcasting a steady stream of intuitive insights. He was constantly on the go: pondering, observing, testing, driven by that inner urge to do something no one else had done before.

There was no respite. On top of his gruelling caseload, the headaches returned with a renewed vengeance, with a severity that, literally, would knock him unconscious. And he began to develop physical problems, like water on the lungs and a motor deficiency in his right leg. But he kept on working, going to the practice on crutches, telling his patients he'd twisted his ankle at tennis or tripped and fallen down the stairs.

Even at night there was no rest. Over a four-year period – between 1975 and 1979 – he'd regularly awaken in the morning to find his desk covered with cryptic notes and curious drawings, scrawled while he thought he slept. Or he would be told he'd been raving in his sleep in some unknown tongue. A girlfriend at the time actually recorded one of these night-time sessions and took the tape to the speech laboratory at the University of Heidelberg. All the experts could say was that it sounded like an old Cantonese dialect from imperial China.

Fortunately, he always kept these nocturnal scribblings. And often, weeks or months later, they would reveal the key he needed to unravel a puzzle or take the next step in perfecting a system.

It was precisely in this way, he told Verena and me, that he discovered a missing link in his EEA diagnostic system.

He was still assessing Kirlian phenomena individually, in detail – what this single fly-away point indicated, what that particular cluster of points was saying – when he decided, one evening, to bring some order to the chaos littering his desk. And there he came across a bunch of papers, obviously written during one night of delirium, that had to do with a bigger picture, with the overall quality of the radiation.

From the notes he uncovered he realized that basically three distinct *types* of emission qualities existed, and that now, for the first time, he could classify a patient's condition according to disease category.

This discovery provided him with a new and invaluable starting point for diagnosis. By giving a preliminary indication of the genetic disposition and disease group to which a person belonged, the different types of emission qualities pointed him in the right direction far more quickly, giving him an invaluable platform for the subsequent analysis of specific emissions from fingers and toes.

He named the three radiation qualities endocrine, toxic and degenerative.

'Endocrine' emissions, he came to understand, hint at functional disorders like PMS, nervousness, depression, insomnia, headaches; conditions that indicate that the hormone system is out of balance. 'Toxic' emissions show that something aggressive is happening in the body, that the organism is trying to rid itself of toxins, as in enteritis, infections or flu. 'Degenerative' emissions indicate a chronic state of some kind, like gout, persistent fatigue, organ degeneration, rheumatism or arteriosclerosis.

'Many times discoveries came to me like this,' he said. 'My girlfriend would observe me getting up in the night like some sort of moon addict, sitting down at my desk, writing feverishly, and then stumbling back to bed. Often, when I would need some component to complete a system I was working on, I would unearth it there, buried in the clutter on my desk.'

Still, self-doubt gnawed at him: despite travelling to Hong Kong and New Delhi and finding, in both Chinese medicine and Indian ayurveda, solid corroboration for his work; despite seeing the enthusiasm and excitement with which doctors and health practitioners greeted his Kirlian seminars. When he should have been gratified, encouraged, he was overwhelmed by what he called 'the most horrible depressions'.

'Inside, my mind kept asking who I thought I was – me, a simple farm boy, an uneducated metalworker, standing up there in front of all those people, all those doctors and therapists, talking about diagnosis and treatment.

' "What you do may work for you in your practice," my mind would say, "but maybe it won't work for others." It was a very difficult time for me.'

Yet his creativity never deserted him: one innovation followed the next. First came his Acu-Impulse device for moving energy to eliminate blockages and thereby relieving pain; next, his VEGASom machine for harmonizing brainwaves by inducing the brain's own natural beta, alpha, theta and delta rhythms. He even found the time to write, publishing his first book, *Energy Emission Analysis*, at the end of 1983. It was the realization of a profound urge to share his discovery with a wider audience.

One of the most appreciative readers was Josef Angerer, the renowned Jesuit priest and naturopath who founded Germany's biggest and best-known naturopathy school in Munich and, as president of the Association of German Naturopaths in the 1950s, went to battle, and to court, instigating legislation which gave the German *heilpraktiker* the same legal status as a medical doctor.

In Munich, Verena and I hoped to see Angerer, then 86, to talk about Peter Mandel. Unwell at the time, Angerer excused himself, asking his long-time assistant Franz X Kohl, himself a successful naturopath, to speak to us.

Kohl remembered well Angerer's first encounter with Peter Mandel and his Kirlian diagnostic system: 'Even though there were those who negated Peter's work at the time, saying it was all nonsense, Angerer immediately said, "Take note of this man: he is important, he is going to bring dramatic changes." '

Kohl also recalled being present at meetings between the two men. 'Sometimes Josef Angerer would say something nobody understood,' Kohl told us. 'Peter would instantly take up a dialogue with him, and one could really feel they were on the same wavelength. Like Angerer, Peter Mandel walks totally new paths and evolves entirely new thought-models. Like Angerer, he is a revolutionary.

'Before starting my first practice 18 years ago, I assisted at seven different naturopathy clinics, and I know everyone with large practices in Germany,' he added. 'I have to say that Peter Mandel is by far the most creative naturopath in the country: he has completely new ideas; he doesn't just take old concepts and adjust them here and there. In my view, he is a genius phenomenon who, some day, is going to have a place in history like all the big names in natural medicine, like Kneipp and Hahnemann,[1] because he has revolutionized natural healing methods and set them on a modern path.'

For Mandel, the Angerer connection was significant, in more than one respect. 'When I published my book on Kirlian photography, Josef Angerer was one of the first who read it,' Mandel explained. 'Angerer said, "What you are doing is good; it's the future", even when my earlier teachers said it was all stupid games. Being with him, discussing, exchanging ideas, was a great honour for me.'

Second, Angerer helped Mandel come to grips with the term 'God'. Convinced as he was of the soundness of ancient esoteric wisdom, of each individual's potential for self-realization, for enlightenment, for attaining the godhead within, Mandel found the Judaeo-Christian concept of a supreme being impossible to swallow. 'Even though Angerer was a Catholic priest, a monk actually, and expressed himself in the language of a Jesuit scholar, he spoke in a way one would never expect from someone affiliated with an organized religion,' Mandel said. 'Although our language was different, after a short time we recognized that we were actually speaking of precisely the same things. This man influenced me very much in my inner understanding of godliness.'

In 1984, several months after the EEA book appeared in print, the depressions ended as abruptly as they had started. 'They stopped the moment I began to let go,' he recalled, 'when I dropped the habit of asking "Why me?" all the time.

'I had been raised to believe that only educated people were able to reason, but I'd often sat and talked with so-called learned people and had seen that they really know nothing. For the most part – Angerer was a rare exception – their knowledge was static; they were incapable of combining it, of using it to create something new.

'In fact, I began to realize that it was important that I hadn't studied; I would probably have ruined this "farmer's intelligence" I have. Finally, I was able to accept the fact that I am simply good at what I do. And suddenly I felt very free.'

He confesses that he is fully aware of the fact that the theories he expounds and the treatments he demonstrates often seem incredible to others. 'Yet I am in the fortunate position that I don't have to prove them scientifically; science has to prove to me that I'm wrong,' he said. 'It may sound arrogant, but if scientists start examining my work they will see that I'm right. And because they don't want to do this, from the outset they simply state that I'm wrong. But this is actually unscientific, because to be truly scientific would be to examine my statements and try to *prove* them untrue.'

With the cessation of the depressions, the headaches went as well. And, as if his own blocks had been cleared at last, his work with colour really began.

A significant impetus came from a man he'd treated in his practice, the late Professor Gerhard Heuss, a Nuremberg-based architect, teacher and colour consultant. Heuss was fascinated with colour and its effect on man. Researching the science of colour, he'd devoured every arcane text he could find – and was intrigued by the notion of therapeutically incorporating colour into modern architecture to make living and working environments more harmonious.

There were parallels, of a sort, in history. In Hermopolis, the Egyptian city that preceded Alexandria, it is said that Thoth, the ruler, had the city laid out in the shape of the zodiac and, at its heart, commanded a Pharos-like tower[2] to be constructed. From this central lighthouse, individual colours of the spectrum were supposedly radiated over different sections of the city, influencing the temperament of each sector's inhabitants and, together, creating a harmonious whole.

For Heuss, colour was also a means to an end, a vehicle for triggering a sense of harmony in those who occupied his buildings.

'I have nearly all Professor Heuss's unpublished texts – he gave them to me – and they helped lay the foundation for what I do today,' Mandel told us. 'I had also read all the other colour researchers, Babbit, Langsdorf, Goethe and the rest, and it was as if it all mingled in my head and suddenly things fell into place, like in those gambling machines where you get three oranges in a row and, *clang, clang, clang*, the money comes out.'

Since light is energy and our bodies are also energy, he reasoned that there must be a correlation. 'Our cellular structure is based on light, as Popp has proven, and colours are also light – and that's why I can use this medium, colour-light, to repolarize imbalances, to make disharmonies harmonious.' And harmony, in terms of natural medicine, is synonymous with health.

Initially, he experimented with an existing therapy, VitaColour. It called for coloured filters to be fitted on to huge lamps, and then for patients to sit in front of them for an hour or more. The Kirlian photos revealed excellent results, but Mandel found the process too unwieldy. Plus it took too long.

From his earlier work in therapeutic massage, and the successes he'd had in relieving pain by massaging certain points on the body – like in his first complete system for treating sciatica, the one that came to him driving home from his Heidelberg practice – he realized that *points* should be irradiated with colour, not whole areas of the body.

He developed a makeshift cylinder with a flat lens about the size of a beer bottle cap. But it took from ten to 15 minutes per point before there was any reaction from patients. 'It wasn't at all satisfactory. We could only irradiate three to six points in an hour.'

And then, as it tended to happen, his finely honed intuition came through once again.

He'd accepted a dinner invitation from the director of VEGA, the Black Forest-based company which manufactures his Kirlian machines. As Mandel left his office that evening, he noticed a small pyramid on his desk. Without thinking, he popped it into his pocket.

'During dinner, before knowing what I intended to say or why, I suddenly retrieved the pyramid from my pocket and placed it on the table. "Mr Grieshaber," I heard myself saying, "this pyramid shape is exactly what I need for applying the colour. I need coloured glass rods with a pyramid focus, and a torch-like affair with the light in the back." '

'Later, when we had a prototype, I tried it out and found that only one minute's irradiation was required before the reaction came. And that was the birth of the Colourpuncture tool we use to this day.'

A second significant realization was to follow before Colourpuncture really took off, before new systems presented themselves, one after another, with breathtaking speed. This time, the Acu-Impulse device he'd developed in the late 1970s provided the stimulus.

'I used to go to exhibitions and set up a stand to demonstrate the apparatus, telling people that if they had pain I could make it disappear quickly,' he explained. 'Depending on where the pain was in the body, I'd apply the Acu-Impulser to the appropriate acupuncture points on the holographic microsystem on the ear, and with several short impulses the pain would be gone.

'I realized that with the Acu-Impulser I was giving a spark that moved the blocked energy and relieved the pain, but I was simply moving the energy as it was, without changing the content. And I had the gut feeling that, for the healing *process* to be initiated, the bio-information carried by that moving energy also had to be changed.'

At this point in time, as Mandel was mulling over the mysteries of informative energy, he encountered the concept of cybernetics, developed by the American mathematician Norbert Wiener and named after the Greek word *kybernétés*, meaning 'steersman'.

Cybernetics is the science of controlling the direction of a process. Industrially, the cybernetic approach was applied to the development of 'intelligent' robots to perform certain functions like inserting tiny components into circuit boards on an assembly line, as well as the creation of 'decision-making' machines to run fully automated factories. The idea is that there is an overriding software program, a 'steersman', guiding the process by communicating the correct data required for each step.

In terms of man and the cosmos, the cybernetic attitude compares the universe to a gigantic, intelligent computer of coded data programs, with data transmitted via such electromagnetic waves as cosmic rays and light.

One of the most important exponents of this view was the cybernetician Dr David Foster. In *The Intelligent Universe*, published in 1975, he wrote: 'The total universe, inclusive of all aspects of matter and mind, shows a construction virtually indistinguishable from that of an electronic computer, and all its workings are in the nature of intelligent data processing.'

It was the notion of coded data, of information being transmitted by various forms of radiation – like light – that struck a chord with Peter Mandel. 'Cybernetics fitted exactly with the way I'd been thinking,' he stated. 'Here we have the impulse, which is energy, and here we have colour, which is information. The frequency of an energy is information, and the carrier of this frequency is the energy. Of course one cannot separate these, but still they are two entities, like the right and left shoes that make up a pair.

'And that's how Esogetics began.'

As usual, existence's timing was apropos. So much had happened, and kept on happening, that he needed a model to contain it all. By now he'd developed the Kirlian-based EEA diagnostic system, the Acu-Impulser, the VEGASom machine and a range of Colourpuncture systems (including the first four circles of the Transmitter Relays) as well as Coloursound therapy, whereby, working with musicians Ludovika Helm and Kay Korten, he'd managed to convert the frequencies of certain Colourpuncture systems on to therapeutic music cassettes. It was time for an overriding canopy, an umbrella; it was time to set down his own unique perspective on the processes of life.

There were two worlds to bring together, the inner and the outer, the esoteric and the energetic. He wanted to fuse the wisdom of the ancients with the advances of modern science.

His angle, his standpoint, was medical, focused on man and his well-being. But there was also a greater goal. Not only did Mandel want to alleviate the ailments of those who came to him, he wanted, essentially, to help prevent disease.

A statement made during a seminar, years later, succinctly illustrates the spirit that moved him. 'All over the world, in spring and autumn, flu-related infections hit 60 per cent of people,' he said. 'The whole medical profession jumps on this 60 per cent, but nobody bothers about the remaining 40 per cent because they're not sick. If I were a scientist I would jump on this 40 per cent. I would, in fact, ask why this virus does not hit this 40 per cent. If I could get to the bottom of why it is like this, then I could help the 60 per cent – beforehand.'

Visually, he symbolized his Esogetic philosophy by placing two triangles tip to tip (figure 6). The upper triangle represents esoteric wisdom, the sum total of all mankind's knowledge of the subtle, the unseen; the lower triangle, the most recent findings of biophysics, as well as the philosophies of cultures like the Chinese and Hindu, in so far as they relate to the body and the processes of life. 'At the melting point of these two triangles something new comes into being,' he said: 'Esogetics.'

In relation to his Esogetic thought-model, the most significant reality expressed by the esoteric triangle is 'As above, so below' – in other words, macrocosm equals microcosm, with everything, from planets and plankton to pine trees and people, governed by the same universal laws.

Credit for first bringing this insight to mankind's attention goes to Hermes Trismegistos who, sometime between AD 100–300, wrote the *Hermetica*, a collection of theses said to contain the quintessence of all knowledge.

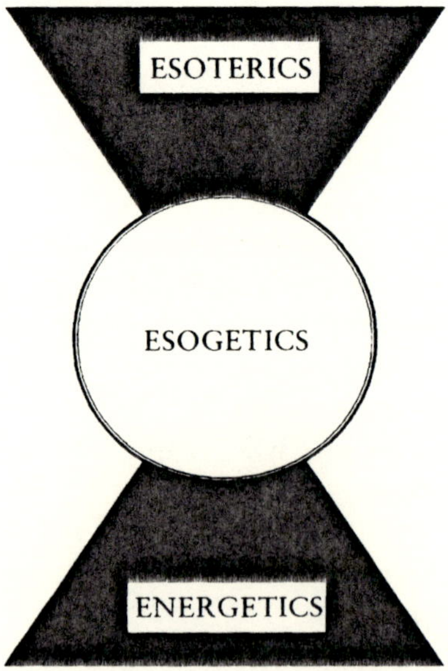

Figure 6 The Esogetic principle

The *Hermetica* was considered, by early European scholars, to have been divinely inspired, and Hermes Trismegistos himself is generally thought to have been an Egyptian adept, an alchemist. In fact, during the Middle Ages, he came to be known as the 'patron saint' of alchemy.[3]

The words that resonated so strongly with Peter Mandel are from an early alchemical text of Trismegistos known as the *Emerald Tablet*. 'That which is above is like to that which is below,' it says, 'and that which is below is like to that which is above.'

The most obvious illustration of 'As above, so below' is to be found in the fact that the structure of the largest 'unit' in our world, the solar system, is replicated in the smallest, the atom. At the centre of our solar system is the star we call the sun, around which the planets orbit. At the heart of the atom is a central nucleus (of protons and neutrons) around which electrons, the basic particles of electricity, orbit. Energy and light are produced at the sun's core by the nuclear fusion of hydrogen and helium, and by 'splitting the atom' – by duplicating this same process of nuclear fusion – mankind has learned how to release the energy of the atom and transform it into a weapon of war. And scientists have only been able to do so because of the universal truth of this axiom, because of 'As above, so below'.

I also find it illustrated in the fact that I once experienced the light at the centre of my being, and that Dr Popp discovered that light exists at the core of our every cell. And I hear it in language, when we speak of how we feel. When daylight is gone we say 'night has fallen'; when our spirits plummet we call it 'the dark night of the soul'. To me this is not just metaphor; this is a mirroring of a natural outer phenomenon, manifesting inside us in precisely the same way. I am also of the opinion that 'As above, so below' was exactly what the authors of the Bible meant when they stated that man had been made in the image of the creator.

Here, in more current terminology, is the same truth expressed by David Foster in *The Intelligent Universe*: 'The universe is a total construction of waves and vibrations whose inner content is "meaning", and man is a microsystem of the same vibratory nature floating at some depth in the universal and meaningful wave system.'

Esoterics is more than a philosophy, however. At its essence, it is a homing device, a pointer towards the truth of who we really are. 'As above, so below' is, then, a light on the path. Once this understanding penetrates, anything external – from sunset to cyclone, criticism to kiss – becomes a mirror for our conditioned programs and emotional processes, our hidden fears and secret aspirations; an outer reflection of one's inner self. And like coins in a piggy bank, these little moments of awareness add up. As Lao Tzu is reported to have said: 'A journey of a thousand miles begins with a single step.'

Colourpuncture, I have seen from my own experience, supports this process of awakening. And in some people, it even seems to trigger it. Mandel told us that many patients, after a series of Colourpuncture treatments, report a sudden, out-of-character interest in spirituality and meditation.

The lower triangle, symbolizing energetics, embodies the new and the old – the energy system of Chinese medicine (including those of the Egyptians, Hindus, Greeks, Romans and other early civilizations) as well as the discoveries of present-day pioneers, like the work of biophysicist Fritz-Albert Popp documented in earlier chapters.

Although Mandel's Esogetic Model was formulated in the 1980s, it is to his credit that it has not dated in any way. Testifying to the totality of his understanding of man as an energy being is the fact that every new discovery of Popp's, for example, and the findings of quantum physics – like David Bohm's holographic theory of the universe – are effortlessly absorbed.

To illustrate: In *The Holographic Universe* Michael Talbot writes, 'One of Bohm's most startling assertions is that the tangible reality of our everyday lives is really a kind of illusion, like a holographic image. Underlying it is a deeper order of existence, a vast and more primary level of reality that gives birth to all objects and appearances of our physical world in much the same way that a piece of holographic film gives birth to a hologram.'

Is this not further confirmation of the age-old principle, 'As above, so below'? It also exemplifies a turnaround that we are witnessing more and more these days, as progressive scientists, particularly quantum physicists like David Bohm, arrive at conclusions expounded by mystics for centuries. The Hindu sages who wrote the Upanishads some ten thousand years ago may not have used the word 'holographic', yet they said the same as Bohm, that our 'tangible reality' is *maya*, illusion.

In the early 1980s Mandel wasn't using the word 'holographic' either, but he certainly understood the holographic concept that the part contains the whole. Peter Mandel already knew that the total life information of every living thing is carried in each and every one of its cells.

'The sensational experiment of the biologist Gordon, who removed the content of a frog's ovum and replaced it with material from an intestine cell, and then induced this cell to divide, has confirmed that each cell carries the overall program of the organism,' he wrote in *Esogetics*. 'From one intestine cell, a fertile frog was created! This miracle – the creation of a clone – is the proof.'

DNA is additional evidence of an informational program. Today, it's common medical knowledge that data carried in the DNA determines body structure, from hair of brown and eyes of blue to lean or stocky thighs. Or a predisposition to certain physical weaknesses or sicknesses.

But Mandel had his vision set on greater heights. If life information is carried in each cell and in each person's DNA, if 'As above, so below' is an eternal truth, does it not follow, he reasoned, that there is also an information blueprint for each individual life? He concluded that everyone who comes into this world must do so carrying completely detailed information according to a fixed plan.

'Development, growth and all other functions are preprogrammed,' he declared in *Esogetics*. 'How can one then doubt that the program of one's own life course exists in a structured matrix? Even today, however, this still sounds too metaphysical to be acceptable.

'Imagine that each evolutionary stage is pre-programmed at the time of birth. Then each person's entire life path would be prerecorded from the very beginning. Our intellectual brain, our mind, cannot conceive of this so easily. In spite of this, we consistently know and sense that there is something that guides us, yet eludes our mind's grasp. This "something" is certainly there, and the analytical mind strives to understand it.'

Frankly, had I encountered the idea of this 'something', of a life program, before meditation entered my life, I must confess I would have found Mandel's statements difficult to accept. But I have seen that a blueprint does indeed exist, and that it is accessible. It is inscribed, for example, on the palms of our hands. It is also decipherable through astrology – confirming, for me, Mandel's assertion that the life program is imprinted at the moment of conception and that the information it carries is activated by birth.

Does this mean we are victims, slaves to some hidden cosmic plan? Not at all.

Life, say the mystics, is a cosmic classroom, and graduation is enlightenment, the conscious return to the source. They also say, along the way, that we incarnate again and again; and that, between incarnations, our spirits choose the precise womb, the exact situation in which to acquire the experience that will teach us the lessons we are coming here to learn.

'You have been born many times, you have died many times, but you have continued,' said Osho in *The Transmission of the Lamp*. 'And *all* your experiences, as far as your evolution of consciousness is concerned, are with you. That is the only possibility for man some day to become enlightened, because even if he gets a few steps closer each life towards the truth, one day he is going to reach home.'

Esogetic medicine, Mandel contends, can take us 'a few steps closer' from wherever we are.

'If we can recognize the meaning hidden behind pain and suffering, we can turn on our heels and abandon the path that leads to the void,' he wrote. 'If we do not recognize this, then pain and disease become meaningless. Then we have not understood the signal and the message that says, "Turn around, change your actions and realize yourself." Our downfall is predetermined.

'The Esogetic Model gives man the possibility to "take himself in hand" – especially at times of apparent health – in order to experience the divine energy within . . . Its purpose is to attempt to experience the centre through the body.'

Mandel's Esogetic Model

Peter Mandel's Esogetic Model comprises seven aspects – he calls them molecules – arranged in an outer circle around a central core (figure 7).

The three lower molecules belong to our material world; the upper three, to the higher realms of being. The central molecule, the Transcendental Field, symbolizes the divine spark that resides in each of us. Just as a wave is separate yet indivisible from the ocean, this spark, this light at our centre, is part and parcel of the very source that is the origin and sustenance of the energy called life.

As we progress through the molecules of the Esogetic Model, it is interesting to note Mandel's use, time and again, of the number 'seven'. Equated with wisdom in numerology, 'seven' stamps many aspects of our existence – seven days of the week, seven colours, seven notes in the musical scale, seven chakras, the seven-year cycles that are the milestones of our lives.

The first molecule of the Esogetic Model is Body Systems. It views the physical body as matter which must be brought to life – comparing it to computer hardware which, until it is activated by software, cannot function.

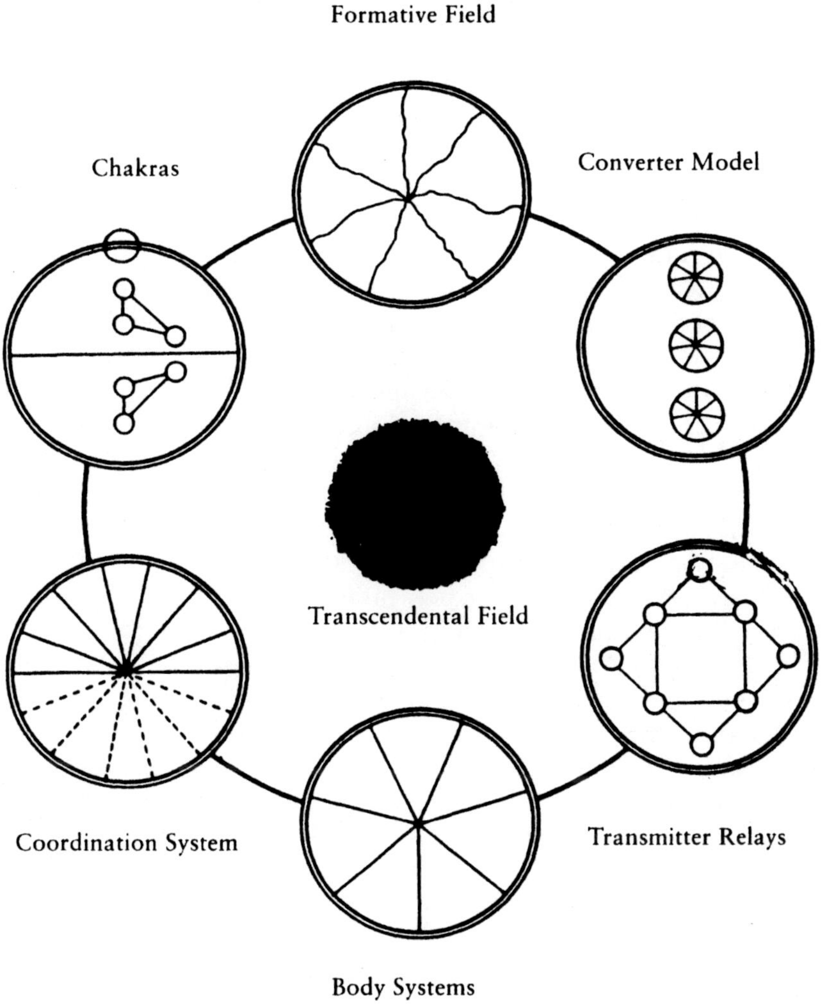

Figure 7 Esogetic Model

Software programs are basically instructions that cause the hardware to do the work we require, from word processing or database management to a myriad other tasks. With software, the operative word is 'instructions' and the same can be said of the human body. Everything is in place – cells are organized into organs and systems, awaiting the information that, carried on the energy, will bring the physical form to life.

Through Mandel's eyes, physical matter is a 'spectral' unity, with each cell grouping vibrating at a specific frequency, expressible in one of the seven colours of the spectrum. Ancient cultures knew this, he is certain, since early texts on colour therapy carefully pinpoint the alliance of particular colours with specific organs and systems. Historically, for example, the vibration of red correlates to the functional frequency of the 'cell groupings' we know as the heart, lungs, muscles, bones and kidneys.

He concluded, then, that all organ systems are governed by colour aspects, and that imbalances could be harmonized by irradiation with the very colour in which these organ systems intrinsically vibrate. And this, he subsequently discovered, happens via the body's inbuilt communications system, the cellular network with its language of light.

Although each cell possesses our entire life information – as Gordon's creation of a new frog from an intestine cell proves – it still has its appointed task to fulfil, its own contribution to make to the living whole. Obviously, coordination is required.

Coordination is the role of Mandel's second molecule. The Coordination Systems, housed in the brain, distribute instructions to the farthest reaches of our beings, provoking specific responses in accordance with the master plan.

Mandel assigns this coordination function to seven organs in the brain, the 'Council of Seven', as he dubbed them. Although they do not represent the sum total of the brain's function, Mandel selected these seven organs because each plays a key, and equally meaningful, role in coordinating body processes. The nobles of his Council of Seven are the thalamus opticus, the hypothalamus, the hypophysis or pituitary gland, the epiphysis or pineal gland, the limbic system, the corpus callosum (the bridge between the brain's right/left hemispheres and upper/lower parts) and the medulla oblongata.

Despite generations of dedicated research, the intricacies of the human brain still rank among nature's best-kept secrets. Many mysteries have been solved, however, and are well documented in scores of books – and for the reader wishing for an extensive account of the functions of these seven coordination organs, I suggest a copy of Mandel's *Esogetics* or a visit to the local library. For the reader who, like me, is simply a fascinated layman, here are a few insights into how this Council of Seven, seated at the apex of the information pyramid, manages the systems of this mind/body complex in which our spirits are housed.

The thalamus opticus is like a telephone switchboard at the gateway to consciousness. It routes inner 'calls' like pain, and outer stimuli like temperature, to the highest part of the brain so that we can respond – by figuring out why we're hurting or that we need a sweater because it's getting cold. It also controls such basic emotional reactions as like and dislike, and reflex actions like 'fight or flight'.

The hypothalamus's major responsibility is to supervise and regulate the release, into the bloodstream, of hormones produced by the hypophysis or pituitary gland. It also governs the body's acid/alkaline balance, makes us sweat if it's hot, keeps us breathing regularly, and controls the part of the nervous system that regulates involuntary muscles, like automatically slowing the heart rate while we sleep.

The hypophysis secretes hormones to regulate body processes like growth, salt and water metabolism, egg and sperm production and, in new mothers, the generation of milk. Hormones also affect our emotions strongly; for example, such hormonal processes as puberty or menopause are often accompanied by psychological stress.

The epiphysis or pineal gland controls the action of light on the body by secreting melatonin, a hormone which regulates the body's 'inner clock', and produces, if in a state of imbalance, conditions like insomnia or extreme fatigue. In esoteric literature, the pineal is known as the gland of light, the 'third eye', the seat of intuition, the eye of the soul.

Although it performs certain biochemical functions as well, the limbic system's most interesting role is linking the body and the emotions. Our response to smells provides the best illustration: we feel alarm at the smell of smoke, are revolted by the smell of decay, or, like Marcel Proust in *A la recherche du temps perdu* (Remembrance of Things Past), are instantly reconnected to moments of childhood happiness by the smell of baking *madeleines*.[4]

The sixth coordinator is the corpus callosum, the information carrier between right-side brain functions of emotion and spatial perception, and left-side rational, intellectual, mathematical and analytical thinking.

Mandel said he first became aware that information was being exchanged via the corpus callosum when he identified laterality disturbances in patients' Kirlian photographs. 'Imbalances in information exchange result in a cramping in the area of the corpus callosum, which will, in turn, affect the coordination organs, the thalamus, hypothalamus and pituitary,' he said. 'The information contained in the impulses transmitted by the coordination organs to the periphery, to body organs and systems, is altered, and coordination errors result.' Such as learning difficulties in children.

The final coordination organ in the Council of Seven is the medulla oblongata, controlling such vital functions as respiration, heart rate and circulation. It is also the centre for vomiting.

The medulla, Mandel observed, also has a direct connection to the solar plexus, and this led him to develop a simple technique for relieving tension or pain caused by stress or fear, and felt in the stomach. Just by pressing on a medulla reflex zone at the back of the head, discomfort can quickly be relieved.[5]

The Esogetic Model's third molecule is the seven Transmitter Relays. Essentially, the Transmitter Relays are about transferring power to body processes and, as well, about filtering, from the influx of cosmic energy, the specific information required for each life program to unfold. Mandel likens the Transmitter Relays to Cerberus of Greek mythology, the guard dog at the entrance to the underworld.

In earlier chapters, I have already written about the Transmitter Relay I experienced, the Relay of Memory. The other six are responsible for cellular information, instinct and functions of the immune system.

With the fourth molecule, the Chakras, we enter the subtle dimensions of being. In Mandel's model, the chakras are centres of pure, spiritual information, independent of time and space; he sees them as the organizational model of life itself. They are our individual Akashic record, our own personal file in the cosmic database.

The fifth Esogetic molecule, the Converter Model, reflects Mandel's understanding that, in this dimension, information cannot exist on its own, but is always in partnership with energy – and this insight led him to the discovery of three invisible suns or 'energy converters' situated in the head, chest and belly. Like power stations, their job, 24 hours a day, is to produce energy for body processes.

Despite the fact that these converters have nothing to do with information, he discovered how to use them to relieve pain as well. The impetus, he said, came from the statement of Dr Reinhard Voll that pain is the outcry of the tissue for a flood of energy.

Using 'seven' as a basis for calculation, he identified 147 'Converter Points' on the skin, each related to a specific body sector – and found that if there was pain in one of these sectors it could be quickly relieved by a short, intense pressure of the thumb on the related point.

A small illustration: a couple of years ago, Verena, who is a trained physiotherapist, was filling in at the practice of a vacationing friend. A woman came with such pain in her knee that she couldn't straighten her leg. Verena decided to try manipulating Mandel's Converter Point for the knee on the shoulder. With her thumb, she exerted a short, hard burst of pressure – and the pain disappeared. The woman, Verena told me, left the session walking normally, shaking her head in disbelief, trying to figure out how Verena had fixed her knee by pressing on her shoulder!

The sixth molecule of the Esogetic Model is Mandel's Formative Field, the form-giving force he compares to the morphogenetic field of Rupert Sheldrake. Not only does the Formative Field contain all the primary information of this dimension, it is also the first point of entry of the spiritual into the material. And through this connection to universal information we experience the individual life plan that exists for us exclusively, for each of us and for each of us alone. It is the plan life is constantly reminding us to fulfil.

The Formative Field is also the birthplace of thought. 'Here, thought comes into being,' Mandel wrote in his latest book, *Colours: The Pharmacy of Light*. 'Together with the information it is carried by the energy, filtered through the Transmitter Relays, passed on to the coordination organs and, finally, becomes reality in the physical body.'

At times, when writing, I sense this process at work. It is the experience I mentioned at the beginning of this chapter: of form manifesting out of the formless, of being what Zen calls a hollow bamboo.

When this happens, I have observed that the mind is silent, and that the words originate somewhere else. I feel them arising in the middle of my chest and then, through my typing fingers, manifesting on the computer screen. Afterwards, there is never any sense of ownership, of them having been written by 'me'.

What I am witnessing, I reckon, is Mandel's Formative Field at work – with pure thought, unadulterated by the manoeuvrings of my mind, being carried on the energy of the Converter in my chest and then, through the coordination functions of my brain, taking form in this dimension.

The same process happens with sickness. Remember the statement of the Chinese master that disease is a thought? Or the following insight by physicist F David Peat in his study of the North American Indian 'worldview', *Blackfoot Physics*: 'Disease is a manifestation of human thought because it is ideas, worldviews, and beliefs that create the conditions in which a society can be riddled with disease, strife, and poverty, or can continue in health and harmony.'

In chapters to come, through stories of people and their illnesses, we will see how conditioned ideas, borrowed beliefs and unresolved conflicts – all thoughts – can, unless transformed, manifest as sickness on the physical plane.

'Unless the negative patterns locked in the body are erased, the higher energies are blocked from penetrating this dimension,' Mandel said. 'And we can never live our lives to their full potential.'

The Transcendental Field, the radiating sun at the centre of his Esogetic Model, is the final molecule. And here Mandel, rarely at a loss for answers, is left with questions.

'How can one describe something which exists beyond space and time?' he asked in *Esogetics*. 'How can one understand that polarity arose out of an "all-one"? Is this concept beyond the reach of man's mind? I believe that the spark of the spirit in all that lives carries, within itself, the answer to the question of the transcendental.' And if the answer eludes him in this incarnation, he said he hopes to come back and ask again.

This, then, is a glimpse into Mandel's Esogetic Model, his synthesis of the wisdom of the ancients and the advances of modern man.

In my view, Mandel's contribution couldn't be more timely: I see the informative-energetic medicine of Esogetics as *the* medicine for the next millennium. And I believe people are ready.

Had I spoken to my late father about 'energy' and 'information' he would have stared back at me blankly. But we are the children of a different age. With his discoveries about energy, Einstein altered the course of modern science completely. He opened our minds to new possibilities, to the point where we can now incorporate ideas that would once have been thought outlandish, like David Bohm's holographic universe or Fritz-Albert Popp's cellular communication through impulses of light.

And thanks to computers and the software that drives their programs, the same can be said about information. Now we can easily assimilate the concept of information in relation to our own bodies and beings – whether we're talking about DNA or Mandel's life program. Times have changed: to my father, 'information' was news he gleaned from his morning newspaper.

Around the world, growing numbers of people are welcoming the spiritual into their lives. They're meditating, reading the mystics, delving into the mysteries of ancient cultures. They're hungry for something higher, ready to put time-honoured truths into practice to enrich their lives.

Peter Mandel has synthesized yesterday and today, and created the possibility of a new tomorrow, free from physical disorders and psychological dis-ease. By giving us a comprehensive blueprint of man's energy and information systems – and complementing it with practical Colourpuncture treatments – he illustrates how, through the medium of the body, we can activate the light of consciousness, the greatest healing power of all.

6

Holographic healing

A science to be a science
must be capable of manifestation
on every plane of consciousness;
in other words
it must be capable of demonstrating the axiom
'As above, so below'.
ARCHIBALD COCKREN

Points, lines, arcs, triangles, squares, rhombi, ellipses – at a Colourpuncture seminar the shapes of geometry fill the overhead screen. But we're not talking dimensional mathematics here: Mandel's figures are systems for treatment, inscribed on the map of the human skin.

'Where there is matter, there is geometry,' deduced the 17th-century German mathematician and astronomer Johannes Kepler when he discovered that planets orbit in ellipses around the sun. And after years of observation and intuition, guided by the precept 'As above, so below', Mandel discovered a geometry of energy, a geometry for healing, imprinted on the surface of the skin.

These ellipses and squares and triangles may be invisible to the eye, but three decades of clinical results confirm they exist. Mandel has shown that by irradiating these geometric forms with coloured light – the points that define them or their outlines, with precise colours and in a prescribed sequence – he can influence physical and psychological processes. There's a rhombus on the back, for example, for stimulating the lymphatic system; a triangle on the face for draining clogged sinuses; a square on the belly for easing sore backs; an ellipse on the buttocks for heightening perception and another on the skull for expanding consciousness. And from head to foot, tip to toe, there are a myriad of others; hundreds and hundreds more.

The turn-of-the-century Italian physician, professor and researcher into the paranormal Guiseppe Calligaris also described these squares and triangles and rhombi. He called them *placche*, plaques, and concluded that they were traces left on the skin as energy moves from within to without, much like embarrassment produces blushing or a food allergy is expressed externally in an outbreak of hives.

These geometric configurations are created by the intersection of subtle energy channels – the vertical acupuncture meridians of Chinese medicine (actually proven in 1989, by one Professor V P Kaznacheev of Russia, to be circuits of light), the electro-acupuncture networks of Dr Voll, and a number of hitherto undiscovered horizontal and diagonal energy streams Mandel himself identified through analysing Kirlian photographs. Like rivers of information, these energy lines traverse the body inside and out, criss-crossing each other, creating an etheric grid upon which light quanta move.

In terms of treatment, the function of the figures formed by these crossovers, Mandel believes, is to 'brake' the flow of light, creating an opportunity for the information inherent in the light wave to be then introduced, via the energy-conducting meridians, to specific body systems.

The concept of an energy gridwork is an ancient one, not only in relation to man, but also (and true to the principle of 'As above, so below') to the earth upon which we live, as well as to the very cosmos which gives us life.

Our planet is energetically nourished by its own system of meridians, by a grid of subtle channels called ley lines. Ancient and indigenous cultures knew of them – Australia's Aborigines still speak of 'songlines' – but today, for the most part, they've been relegated to myth. But not by the Chinese. Whether building a home in Hong Kong, erecting an office block in Shanghai or opening a shop in Sydney's Chinatown, a *feng-shui* expert is generally consulted to determine if a proposed site is suitable, if it's in harmony with the currents coursing through the earth.

Mystics describe an even greater grid, an invisible network of energy lines that permeates the whole of space. This is the 'ether' of the early Greeks, the medium of travel for light and other electromagnetic radiation. It is also the universal web out of which frequencies crystallize into matter – like the human Formative Field of Mandel's Esogetic Model, but on a grander, cosmic scale.

'A snow crystal can form itself instantly when a given condition of temperature and pressure is present,' wrote Vera Stanley Alder in *The Secret of the Atomic Age*. 'But how does it take its perfect and often complicated, and always true, shape? Obviously that form must be in the atmosphere, as it can be nowhere else. There must be some stratum of the atmosphere which is holding forms, forms everywhere, radiating in every direction . . .

'These extraordinary facts in nature, and many others, prove to us that the invisible (to us) atmosphere contains a network of radiant forms or moulds, to which grosser matter clings as it congeals . . . Thus a vast interlacing web would be formed in which energies or activities or substances are gradually stepped down or transmuted from the highest source of life through to the most solid and "inert", or "matter." '

Mandel's Esogetic Model and Colourpuncture systems imply a clear grasp of the structure and function of this cosmic grid – but it is the individual's own private etheric template, and the therapeutic potential it contains, that is his prime focus of attention, his principal field of work.

'People who see auras describe this grid as a cloud,' Mandel said. 'I believe this cloud is the merging of our energy bodies integrating on to the surface of the body. And I am convinced that all the information of our life is contained here – spiritual, mental, emotional and physical. The result is a kind of cosmic compendium, a manual of the person's informative energies, of his or her predetermined life processes, etched on the skin.'

It would seem, then, in deciphering the riddle of our largest organ, that the great majority of us are still scratching the surface. Yet, if quizzed about our skin, we could all undoubtedly muster a few astute observations. We might say it's washable and waterproof, that it sweats to cool us, and that it heals itself if it's hurt. We might also say it's rosy when we're healthy, or that when we're under the weather it turns a ghostly shade of pale.

But there's a great deal more. Not only does the skin automatically reveal how we physically feel, it mirrors our emotions too. Our cheeks redden when we're bashful, we get goose-flesh when we're startled, and anxiety makes us sweat. Conversely, the skin is also a vehicle for triggering emotion. A caress can make us loving, a slap can provoke anger, and a dip in a lake on a hot summer's day can fill us with delight.

A significant but less apparent characteristic is that the skin is capable of conducting an electric current – which is why, walking across a synthetic carpet and touching a metal doorknob, sparks fly and we get a mild electric shock.

It is due to this same reason – because it is an electric field – that the skin has the capacity to communicate information about our thoughts and feelings. Even though we might often prefer to conceal emotions like fear or embarrassment, our skin exposes us ruthlessly. This is because each inner emotional reaction produces an outer electric charge on the skin – and not only are the effects of these charges visible to others, they can also be measured. This is the principle behind the lie-detector test, and Mandel's Kirlian machine.

The skin is also the agency for a broad range of medical treatments – from massage and hydrotherapy to applications of ointments, cold packs or hot poultices. And two popular and well-known skin-based methodologies – Chinese acupuncture and reflex-zone manipulation – contribute to the profusion of healing systems Colourpuncture has to offer.

'Contribute' is the operative word. When I first heard of Colourpuncture I was told (not by Mandel) that it was basically acupuncture with coloured light. I realize now that I was given a simplistic picture, a pat description. Later, speaking to Mandel, I learned that he had indeed studied acupuncture – but not for the system, rather for its empirical knowledge of the meridian network, of the acupuncture grid.

Which explains why, in many of his treatments, we find a mix, a blend of his own geometric figures with the points of traditional acupuncture. The apex of a triangular Colourpuncture system, for example, might be a standard acupuncture point. By the same token, it might well be the point of intersection of a Chinese acupuncture meridian with one of the 14 horizontal energy lines on the body located by Mandel himself.

The reason for his fascination with the acupuncture grid, rather than its systems, is obvious: he had no interest in becoming an acupuncturist, in locking himself into a fixed technique; his vision was fixed on a greater goal. He wanted to do something no one else had done – discover *why* we get sick and find a way to prevent it. And his search led him deep into the realms of man's psyche, to the unspoken thoughts, unexpressed emotions and unlived life lessons where illness really begins.

For Mandel, the acupuncture grid was a door to the body; his own geometric grid, a gateway to higher dimensions, to the realms of mind and spirit, of life programs and cosmic databases. And their functions, he knew, were interrelated, intermeshing, because man is a unity, an indivisible whole.

'I envision grids within grids within grids, just like those little Russian dolls,' he said. 'You open the doll and there's another and then another and another – but you never know there's another unless you move beyond the apparent and take a deeper look.'

And the deeper he delved, the more holographic it all became.

Looking at the effects his geometric systems generate, and their unwavering loyalty to the law 'As above, so below', I am convinced that Mandel's grid is also holographic, that his geometric shapes are reflections of a higher order as yet undefined but, nonetheless, projected on to the skin.

And why not? Physically speaking, acupuncture has already proven the existence of holographic segments on the skin of our bodies.

Consider one of the best-known acupuncture systems, 'the little man in the ear'.

'In 1957 a French physician and acupuncturist named Paul Nogier published a book called *Treatise of Auriculotherapy*, in which he announced the discovery that in addition to the major acupuncture system, there are two smaller acupuncture systems on both ears,' wrote Michael Talbot in *The Holographic Universe*. Although they were actually found by Chinese acupuncturists 4,000 years before, Nogier 'dubbed these *acupuncture microsystems* and noted that when one played a kind of connect-the-dots game with them, they formed an anatomical map of a miniature human inverted like a foetus'.

Today, in countries like China and Korea, this tradition of research continues. As a result, a number of other holographic microsystems have been identified – for example, on the hands, feet, arms, neck, tongue and around the eyes.

Much of the credit for gathering and popularizing these oriental discoveries (or rediscoveries) – and generating greater credence for the holographic paradigm – must go to Dr Ralph Alan Dale, Director of the Acupuncture Education Center in North Miami Beach, Florida. Regularly, through the pages of the *American Journal of Acupuncture*, Dale brings details of newly identified 'micro-acupuncture systems', as he calls them, to the attention of Western acupuncturists.

Yet another holographic system was located by Munich's Dr Jochen Gleditsch, the physician whose 'function circles' figure so predominantly in Colourpuncture diagnosis and treatment. Gleditsch located a network of mouth acupuncture points along the tissue opposite the crowns of the teeth (for which Mandel later developed a Colourpuncture methodology) and was able to prove that the condition of inner organs can be influenced from these points in the mouth.

Gleditsch's 'reflex zones' were new, the principle wasn't – due to the earlier work of an American physician, William Fitzgerald, and an English neurologist, Henry Head.

Fitzgerald located a map of the internal organs on the feet – and subsequently developed the now widely used practice of reflexology – while Head discovered still more reflex zones on other areas of the body.

Take, as a case in point, Head's reflex map on the back. Guided by the knowledge that each organ is nourished by nerve fibres emanating from the spinal cord, and that branches of the same nerves also travel to certain areas on the skin of the back, Head was able to identify reflex relationships with specific organs. There are narrow strips along the spine, near the waist, nerve-linked to the lungs; an ellipse near the right shoulder blade related to the liver; a sausage shape under the left shoulder blade connected to the pancreas; and so on.

Like Fitzgerald, Head found he could 'read' the state of an organ from the condition of its reflex zone on the back and, through massage or manipulation, regulate any dysfunction as well.

Mandel began to treat these reflex zones with colour, with excellent results. And he soon discovered more: a few on the feet – adding to the ten Fitzgerald had already identified – as well as others on the hands, torso and throat.

By treating these reflex zones for the spine and hip joints located on the feet, Lyn White, a reflexologist and Colourpuncturist practising in the Perth suburb of Girrawheen in Western Australia, was able to bring a new freedom of mobility to a 53-year-old woman with lifelong spine and hip pain.

The patient, whom we'll call Marion, had been born with a congenital hip dislocation, and at four years of age had undergone massive surgery to redesign the hip socket and move it some two and a half inches further along her pelvis. 'This left Marion with one hip bone shorter than the other, throwing her posture and balance out completely,' White said. 'When she first came to me for weight loss – because her hips couldn't bear the weight she was carrying – she was suffering from curvature of the spine and arthritis, and was in chronic pain.'

After her weight had been brought down to a comfortable level, Marion asked if Colourpuncture might also help alleviate her hip condition. White turned for guidance to Mandel's *Practical Compendium of Colourpuncture*, and followed his directions for the treatment of diseases of the spine and joints. Among these were the reflex zones.

'After her second treatment, Marion found herself jumping off the table without thinking about it,' White recalled. 'This excited her tremendously; it was something she was normally incapable of doing.

'When she came for the third treatment two weeks later, Marion told me her naturopath had noticed significant changes in her iris during a check-up. She said Marion seemed to have grown taller, that there was more space between her vertebrae and that she was showing signs of regeneration in the entire area from her diaphragm to her knees.'

Today, White said, Marion continues to improve. She is walking taller, has much more energy and experiences no more painful cramping in the hip. 'And one thing fills her with special delight: for virtually the first time in her life, she is able to work long hours in her garden without any pain and stiffness at all.'

Peter Mandel's fascination with reflex zones, however, embraced more than the physical; no matter what his focus at any given moment, there was always that remembrance of the law of higher reflections, of 'As above, so below'. Now, he reasoned, if there are reflex zones on the skin that can influence body processes, there must also be reflex zones related to higher functions, to the psyche, to consciousness. As usual, his hunch paid off; he found precisely what he'd been looking for. It had to do with accessing the life program. And it had to do with dreams.

According to the Esogetic Model, the fourth molecule, the Chakras, is the system responsible for the informative energies of one's life program, for the instructional data of one's own software, as it were. And in Mandel's quest for reflex zones with spiritual connections, he discovered several exhibiting direct relationships to the chakras and, therefore, to the life information of the individual.

The catalyst was the layered-brain model of Israeli researcher P S Rothschild.

According to Rothschild, the upper brain layers rule over the lower, and the lower layers must find a means of release when the hierarchical pressure becomes too strong – from an overabundance of mental activity, for example, induced by anxiety or sorrow or stress. And this release, he maintained, happens through dream pictures.

Rothschild also said that once this inner pressure has been released, the brain layers themselves exchange messages – again in the form of dream pictures.

Mandel was fascinated by the potential of this information exchange as a conduit for informative energies from higher, spiritual levels of being. 'By ridding our beings of mental garbage, dreams free the channels of the brain for the flow of overriding information,' he consequently concluded. 'And then,' he reasoned, logically pursuing his premise, 'if we continue dreaming, our own life information will be revealed, by and by, to our waking consciousness. In other words, we will come into contact with our own life program.'

Time, as usual, proved him right. 'Via the dream zones, we saw that people are indeed able to access their higher selves,' he said. 'We saw that after a certain time, on their own and without any outside pressure, because the flow of information has been freed, they suddenly find they are perceiving more. And then, without knowing why, they begin to come into contact with people and with literature that can help them further on the path towards their true selves.'

From the multitude of 'dream zones' discovered over the years, there are five, in particular, which exhibit a direct connection to the chakras and, therefore, to the life program. These zones are treated at night before going to sleep – first stimulated with a few drops of Mandel's special Esogetic Wild Herb Oil and then irradiated with colour.

Colourpuncture practitioners regularly give dreamwork as homework – which we'll discuss in a subsequent chapter – but for our present purposes here is a short overview of the dream zones relating to the life program. Mandel named them, he said, from the reports of patients who used them over long periods of time.

On the outside of the hip, where it joins the leg, he found a dream zone, about ten centimetres in diameter, that he named the Zone of the Spirit. This zone represents the materialization of the life program and brings us into contact with the overriding spiritual information of our being. Lower, on the inside of the knee, is the Zone of Intuition, for enhancing our intuitive powers and, as a result, assisting us in actualizing the needs of our own spiritual program.

Next is the Zone of Imagination, on the inner ankles. 'Pure intuition is of no help to a person if he cannot translate it into pictures,' Mandel wrote in *Esogetics*. 'Through stimulating this zone, one's power of imagination is strengthened.'

Near the big toe, he found the Zone of Intellect. This zone, he said, 'represents the final stage in this metamorphosis from the spiritual program, via intuition and imagination, to the intellectual understanding of what is released in this process'.

One zone is treated each night – and to promote active dreaming, always in conjunction with the Mental Zone on the back of the upper arm.

There are a multitude more zones, both mystical and mundane. Such as one Mandel assigns to constipation sufferers – as he did with me – to treat at home. Located on the calf above the Achilles tendon, this zone relates to our tendency to cling, to cleave, to hold on tightly. Aptly, he called it the 'Let Go' zone.

There are many other holographic microsystems on various parts of the body, and among the most significant are several Mandel identified for the spine – located on the legs, index fingers, insteps, forehead and, in an inverted position, running down the front of the torso.

The relation of the spine, vertebra by vertebra, to specific organ functions and body processes is well known, particularly in natural medicine, as is the relationship between the spine and mental thought patterns.

'I could not understand why I repeatedly had problems with a stiff neck,' wrote Louise L Hay in her bestselling book *Heal Your Body*. 'Then I discovered that the neck represented being flexible on issues, being willing to see different sides of a question. I had been a very inflexible person, often refusing to listen to another side of a question out of fear. But, as I became more flexible in my thinking and able, with a loving attitude, to see another's viewpoint, my neck ceased to bother me. Now, if my neck becomes a bit stiff, I look to see where my thinking is stiff and rigid.'

Mandel, however, went far deeper. He was able to identify a correlation between present-day spine problems and early psychological traumas – and to resolve the back problem by treating the energy block the childhood shock had produced.

An experience of my own corroborates his findings. At age 40, while making love, a disc in my lower back went out, so badly it took three painful months of chiropractors and osteopaths to get it back into place. The offshoot was a lumbar weakness that troubled me for years. Until the Prenatal therapy I experienced during the Transmitter Relays.

When the disc slipped, my current relationship was in its death throes, and the imminence of its ending was totally freaking me out. I didn't see it at the time, but here was yet another replay of that same old abandonment tape.

According to Mandel's calculations, a back problem at 40 is linked to an unresolved psychological trauma at around five – my age when my second mother died. After the Prenatal therapy helped neutralize the *original* shock that had triggered the pattern in the first place – my natural mother's decision, in her sixth month of pregnancy, to terminate this incarnation – I never had problems with my lower back again. Nor with getting myself into more dead-end relationships.

In addition to childhood or prenatal shocks, countless other factors can warp our natural development – like a woman disowning her femininity because the daddy she adored really wanted a boy. And Mandel discovered a link between spine problems and this unwillingness, or inability, to conform to the overriding feminine (or masculine) principles that bring balance and harmony to our lives.

An example from Rosemary Dass, an Australian-born doctor of oriental medicine currently practising in California, illustrates the use of the spinal hologram on the torso to resolve a physical difficulty and, at the same time, to bring a patient in touch with a higher, psychological imbalance affecting her life.

Dass told me about a woman who came to her with a dislocated neck the morning after a strenuous yoga class. 'Her neck was so badly out she'd lost all enervation down into the first finger which, overnight, had turned a nasty shade of brown,' Dass said. 'She was in a state of total trauma.

'According to Peter Mandel's system, the neck relates to the feminine principle, and the fact that this woman's neck was out points to some conflict around issues of her femininity. But, first, we always start with the body.'

In the inverted-spine hologram found on the trunk of the body, the neck is situated in the area of the navel – and this is where Dass began.

'I treated the points on the belly that relate to the neck, and the pain disappeared immediately,' she said. 'Twenty-four hours later even her finger was back to normal!'

The next day, Dass informed me, the woman returned to the practice, her freshly pink finger exhibited like a trophy, thrilled and amazed at what the Colourpuncture treatment had accomplished. And she wanted more. Today, as I write, Dass and this client have just begun a series of sessions. Together, they're going to delve more deeply into the issue of this woman's femininity, to get to what her neck was really trying to say.

In the California clinic where Dass practises, her colleague is a chiropractor and, as a result, the majority of their clients come, at least initially, with complaints of the spine.

'When people come to the practice with structural difficulties they invariably have problems going on in the unconscious as well,' Dass said. 'But we always have to start where the patient is, where the pain is expressed. And that's in the body.'

The body is the starting point for Mandel's Esogetic Model, and this is the case with Colourpuncture as well. 'If one looks at the hierarchy of Colourpuncture and the other therapies I have developed, the underlying premise is always from the lower to the higher; that is, the way to the top always begins at the bottom,' Mandel stated.

'This means treatment always begins with the cells of the body, where the toxins reside, where the burdens are. First comes the body cleaning, the liberation of the consciousness in the cells – because if the cells are free, then the overriding consciousness becomes freer and freer.'

The healing power of consciousness is a recurring theme in Colourpuncture. It is also a consideration in treatment – because we are all unique, all equal under existence, but in terms of consciousness we are not all the same. No value judgement is intended, but simply look around: there are people whose eyes shine with the light of inner wakefulness, while those of others are dull, sleepy, almost dead.

With consciousness, as with informative-energetic processes,

Mandel takes a hierarchical view. If we do the same, don't we then position the awakened ones, enlightened beings like Buddha or Jesus, Osho or Raman Maharshi, at the top of the ladder? And the rest of us? I reckon we are all heading in the same direction; we're just struggling up our private ladders, at our own speed, rung by rung.

'If someone is sick, we not only have to recognize the person's individuality, we also have to consider the level of consciousness,' Mandel stated. 'We have to ask: "Who is this person? Where is he situated in the hierarchy?"

'Unless a person is ready, I cannot, for example, just attack him with the Transmitter Relays; it could be harmful. Not that the colour could be harmful, but the system could, because I am taking him to a level where he doesn't yet belong.'

And how does Mandel assess the level of consciousness of those who come to him? By a combination of astute observation and, most importantly, by listening to what his patients have to say.

'The majority of doctors and therapists who deal with sick people ask a few questions and then give loads of advice,' he said. 'In other words, the physician uses his own individuality to make the patient conform, because he, the doctor, believes his thinking is right for everyone. And this is not true. That's why I always searched for systems that don't do this. I try not to flood the person with my own thoughts.'

And this approach characterizes the therapeutic relationship as long as it lasts. 'I'm not interested in input; I want output,' Mandel emphasized. 'During and after a Colourpuncture treatment I want the patient to tell me how he is feeling, what sensations he is experiencing, what inner pictures are coming up. Only then can I decide which system to apply next, because it is the patient's reaction to each treatment which guides me, step by step, to the root cause behind the illness.'

Disease, for Mandel, is an impulse for change, a catalyst for introspection and self-assessment; for pinpointing why we're stagnating and then consciously eliminating the cause. From a higher perspective, he views disease as a contravention of one's individual life program; as a straying (for whatever the reason) from one's prearranged path.

'My aim is to give people an impulse that will trigger the search for their own individuality, and to help them do this in a way that doesn't involve talking for years: where people *feel* rather than intellectualize, where the patient realizes he is other than what he thought he was up to now,' he said. 'And the route is from below to above. When we free the consciousness in the cells, we set ripples of consciousness in motion, and eventually they will carry the healing light of awareness to the farthest corners of our being.'

Mandel compares himself to someone who turns the soil of a field that has been lying fallow. 'I only turn the soil; the patient is the one who watches the seeds grow and then reaps the harvest,' he said. 'And that's how he becomes the creator of a new environment, how he begins to live a new life that is healthy, whole, and in harmony with his individual life program.'

The therapist's art

Essentially, a Colourpuncture system is a precision tool, meticulously designed to trigger a specific, yet individual response. And because it is an exact tool, each Colourpuncture system is sacrosanct, not to be amended or adapted, but applied precisely as indicated, colour by colour, point by point.

Deciding which system to use is another question, and this, in effect, is the therapist's art. And today, as an ever-increasing number of health professionals around the world turn to Colourpuncture, Mandel's primary effort is in training practitioners to use his systems in the most effective manner possible.

His vehicle is seminars – week-long residential intensives on a biannual basis, and as many as 40 weekend workshops per year – with simultaneous translation from German into English or Italian, or whatever language is required.

The first step, for a newcomer, is always an introductory seminar on the precepts of Esogetic medicine, on what Mandel describes as 'the Esogetic approach' – and then, building on this base, Kirlian diagnosis and Colourpuncture systems are taught in a structured sequence, in seminars he entitles EEA 1, EEA 2, EEA 3; Colour 1, Colour 2, Colour 3; and so on. And because of Colourpuncture's rapid growth in recent years, particularly internationally, he has now instituted a system of accreditation, with certificates indicating the level of expertise a Colourpuncturist has attained.

For a health practitioner like Dass, who mixes Colourpuncture and Chinese acupuncture; or Franz Kohl, who couples Colourpuncture with homoeopathy and other natural medicines; or Dr Kristen, who uses Colourpuncture exclusively, Mandel has provided an extensive repertoire of systems, of treatment groups from which to choose. There are approximately 200 systems in all, although, at time of writing, he had only taught some 50-odd. The rest are waiting in the wings until the time is ripe.

It is obviously beyond the scope of this book to describe each Colourpuncture system or treatment, what it is for, what it can do – and I refer readers who wish to delve into the treatment cornucopia in greater detail to Mandel's own texts for practitioners, to his *Practical Compendium of Colourpuncture, Volumes 1 and 2*, and to the first volume in a new series designed for the layman, *Colours: The Pharmacy of Light.*

In these books Mandel communicates the basics of Esogetic thought and Colourpuncture and, via illustrations, sets out specific treatments for hundreds and hundreds of common complaints – from acne and bronchitis to constipation and digestion; from frigidity and gastritis to heartburn and influenza; from tonsillitis and ulcers to vomiting and unwanted wrinkles. At first glance, this list may seem to reflect allopathy's focus on symptoms; however, every treatment is holistic in nature and always aimed, whatever the complaint, at seeking out and eradicating the root cause of the disorder.

For a hands-on introduction to Colourpuncture's amazing scope and efficacy, an introductory seminar on Esogetic medicine and some at-home treatments from *Colours: The Pharmacy of Light* are a great way to start.

As far as more serious illnesses or psychological disorders are concerned, Mandel always recommends consulting a professional Colourpuncture therapist. The more complex a disease, and the longer the history, the more intricate the knot that needs to be untied.

Still, for the purposes of this book, I should like to give the reader a general impression of the range of Colourpuncture systems available to practitioners.

First, as I've indicated, come body treatments. These comprise systems for harmonizing endocrine, toxic and degenerative states; for regulating the body's energy currents; for rebalancing the function of organs like the liver or pancreas or spleen.

Next come coordination treatments. These are used for harmonizing functions of the thalamus, hypothalamus, limbic system and the rest of the coordination systems included in this second molecule of the Esogetic Model. In addition, Mandel has designed a series of specific coordination treatments to meet certain criteria, numbering them, simply, 1 to 12.

'The coordination treatments are very comprehensive,' he said. 'They are based on the premise that if the body, at the cellular level, begins functioning as it is supposed to, then one has to bring the coordination systems into balance as well. It's as if there were an earthquake and all the electricity posts fell down. First one has to clean up the mess – which is what the body treatments do – and then rewire.'

Two studies by a prominent Swiss paediatrician show what a doctor or therapist can accomplish by creatively combining treatments from these body and coordination systems.

The studies were conducted by Dr Fausto Pagnamenta, now in private practice in Locarno after 15 years as head of paediatrics at the city's major hospital. His first study dealt with persistent insomnia in children during their first five years; the second, with migraine.

Dr Pagnamenta's childhood insomnia pilot was conducted over a three-year period, and involved 80 children (50 boys and 30 girls) of whom 70 were under three years of age, and the remainder under five.

'All the children included in the study showed symptoms of sleeplessness for at least three months before we began the study,' explained Dr Pagnamenta. 'Twenty-three of the children had difficulty getting to sleep; the other 71 suffered from persistent insomnia, and were waking up three or more times each night. Almost 25 per cent of the children had been prescribed drugs.'

Treatment was simple. Two acupuncture points for the kidneys were irradiated with red, and three points in a coordination combination – comprising acupuncture's Yin Trang (between the eyebrows) GV 20[1] (on the top of the head) and GV 19 (at the back of the head) – were irradiated with violet.

The reason for harmonizing the kidney function, as part of a treatment for insomnia, is linked to the Chinese 'function circle' concept westernized by Dr Jochen Gleditsch. I'm oversimplifying, but, according to Gleditsch, when we begin our life voyage through this dimension the kidney/bladder function circle is where we start. Here the issue is between fear – fear of the dark and of the mother's absence – and the trust that yes, when we awaken, the mother will still be there. By bringing the kidney function into balance with red, the colour of life, the polarity shifts: the fear gives way to the child's innate sense of well-being and trust in existence.

The coordination sequence Dr Pagnamenta employed – the three acupuncture points on the head – is widely used in Colourpuncture. Irradiated with orange, for example, the combination helps dispel moodiness; with blue, it assists in alleviating restlessness. In the insomnia pilot, this sequence was treated with violet – the colour of meditation, as well as, in Mandel's words, 'the colour regulator at the interface between the mind and the body'.

Each Colourpuncture treatment lasted five minutes, with one session every seven to 15 days over a maximum period of four weeks.

And the results? Fifty-six point two-five per cent of the children recovered totally and 37.5 per cent exhibited a marked improvement – a success rate, in terms of recovery *and* improvement, of an impressive 93.75 per cent.

'Colourpuncture proved to be an extremely brief and efficient therapy for childhood insomnia,' concluded Dr Pagnamenta. 'The application of coloured light is simple, harmless and painless, and results appeared within a few days of treatment.

'Needless to say,' he added, 'the parents were thrilled at the prospect of finally getting a good night's sleep.'

Dr Pagnamenta's migraine study ran over four years and included 45 women and 11 men between the ages of nine and 60, with an average age of 40. Of the 56 participants, 49 had migraines so severe they were incapable of functioning during attacks. Migraine frequencies ranged from one every day to 12 'migraine days' a month, over an average span of 14 years. Ninety-four point three-four per cent of the participants took medication to deal with the pain.

In four Colourpuncture sessions or less, 71 per cent of the patients were healed, 26 per cent were better, and there was no change in three per cent of the participants.

The mix of body and coordination treatments is too complex to detail here, but for health practitioners interested in using Colourpuncture to treat migraine – and in evaluating the statistics compiled by Annie Vinter of the Faculty of Psychology at France's University of Dijon – a contact address will be included at the end of this book.

'This success of 71 per cent healed and 26 per cent improved is extraordinary, if one reads the relevant medical literature,' Dr Pagnamenta stated.

Although aware that alternative methods like acupuncture, biofeedback, Alexander technique, relaxation methods and the laying on of hands had also been used to treat migraine, Dr Pagnamenta could not find a single quantitative or qualitative study. The closest he came, he said, was to one conducted by physician and author Dr Oliver Sacks.

'In his book *Migraine*, Sacks describes a study in which one-third of migraine sufferers treated with acupuncture improved, but experienced relapses after treatment was interrupted,' Dr Pagnamenta stated.

'With our study, this did not happen. We observed patients who had been healed at up to four years after the final Colourpuncture treatment, and healing persisted.

'This is also true in relation to one of the most severe cases we studied – a patient who suffered from cluster headaches, with an average of ten attacks every month. We have been observing him for six months now, and since his first and only Colourpuncture treatment he's never had another migraine again.'

In the Colourpuncture hierarchy, after body and coordination systems come a number of systems we've looked at earlier – like Transmitter Relays, Prenatal therapy and the 147 Converter Points.

Then, moving higher, we enter more subtle realms, where even the names of the systems evoke a sense of the mysterious: Sun Lines and Life Streams, Mental Ellipses and Cosmic Clocks. Here, we're talking life programs and cosmic information, incarnational issues and interfacing with the divine – and grasping the dynamics of these systems, and applying them, requires participation in Mandel's most advanced seminars.

In these workshops, Mandel urges doctors, naturopaths and therapists to sharpen their powers of observation and listen attentively to their patients – not influencing their responses, but allowing *them* to say what they are experiencing, what it is they feel. Try to focus on one point, he tells his audience – and that point is the root-cause behind the complaint. And by observing and listening, by applying intelligence, intuition and single-minded focus, the root cause, he assures them, will eventually be revealed.

In the following chapter, we will closely examine a higher system designed to do precisely this, to pinpoint the root cause of a disease and bring it to conscious awareness for resolution. This system is based on the insight that most serious illnesses – like cancer, manic depression, rheumatoid arthritis or Hodgkin's disease, for example – are rooted in emotional conflict. The system is yet another holographic replica – this time on the skull – and it was 'delivered' to Mandel, complete and ready for testing, in a single, visual flash. He calls it Conflict Solving. And as the name promises, it does exactly that.

7

A new paradigm for prevention

An ounce of prevention is worth a pound of cure.
PROVERB

For a thinking, feeling human being, conflict is part of being alive. Emotional conflict of one sort or another is our constant companion, cradle to grave.

The issue, then, is not about eliminating conflict, it's about learning from conflict as it comes along. And it's about finding the courage to face the conflicts that, knowingly and unknowingly, we've buried away, because, as orthodox medicine is now being forced to acknowledge, it is unresolved conflict that makes us sick.

Personally, I gave up expecting a life free of conflict a long time ago. Like it or not, there's no escape: conflict is omnipresent, as existential as summer sun or springtime rain. Male or female, solo or partnered, manager or worker, schoolkid or pensioner, there's emotional conflict wherever human interaction is involved. We encounter it daily, as participant or observer – in our bedrooms and boardrooms; on our television screens and city streets. It's part of the very climate in which we live.

As if outer conflicts weren't enough, there are also those that fester inside us, robbing our sleep and ruining our days. And we all know them well: 'I hate my job but I need the money.' 'This marriage is doomed, but what about the children?' 'No one's ever going to love me; I'll always be alone.' 'I don't understand why, but I'm constantly afraid.' 'I feel like smashing someone all the time!' 'Why can't I have a body like Elle MacPherson?' Et cetera, et cetera.

In truth, these are the real conflicts, these issues of hurt and helplessness, fear and loneliness, anger and self-deprecation – these emotional wounds and self-judgements we want to hide from others and even from ourselves. There are times when suppressing this turmoil seems the only way to survive – but suppression changes nothing; repressed emotions simply weigh us down. And we drag our feet when we could be dancing. Or, in the worst scenario, we end up sick.

Peter Mandel's Conflict Solving therapy is a tool for transforming conflict, for turning it into a gift. Conflict, like experience, is one of life's great teachers. It is one of the fundamental ways life helps us grow.

We looked at illusion in an earlier chapter, at how, in the case of a sunset, what meets the eye isn't what's really going on. And the same is true of conflict.

External conflict is a mirror, an outer reflection of an inner war. Someone may push our buttons, but the buttons are ours. We can explode into blame or implode into shame, but either way we've missed the point. And we've let an opportunity to evolve pass us by.

Colourpuncture's Conflict Solving system is a double-edged sword. On the one hand, it's about preventing illness by learning how to resolve new conflicts as they come along; on the other, it's about purging the past, about cleaning out those shadowy nooks and crannies where ancient conflicts lurk. Because it is here, deep down inside, in the darkness of the subconscious where the seeds of conflict take root and, if left unresolved, can grow into disease.

'Illness begins inside us in very small ways,' Mandel said. 'Conflicts leave traces, no matter how deeply we manage to bury them. Like the lime deposits that, drop by drop, eventually produce stalagmites in caves, these traces accumulate; they get stronger and stronger until, in the end, an organ gets sick. And then the person enters into the arena of official medical care, and a stomach ulcer or diabetes or a swollen liver is diagnosed and treated. But they are only treating the last link in a very long chain.'

In his seminars, Mandel often uses the analogy of a man walking through a darkened room and hitting his head on a chain suspended from a hook in the ceiling. 'Official medicine does nothing but remove the last link in the chain. But if the man walks through the room the next night he's going to hit his head on the chain again,' he stated. 'Conflict Solving helps the patient see that what's actually needed is to take the chain off the hook.'

Mandel's search for a therapy of prevention began many years ago, in the early 1970s, after he'd made the transition from therapeutic masseur to naturopath. At the time, like most practitioners of natural medicine, he was aware of the relationship between emotional conflict and disease. Although Freud, in the 1930s, identified unresolved conflict as a factor in causing mental illness, mainstream medicine continued (and continues) to dismiss any connection between emotion and physical disorders – despite the fact that Chinese physicians documented the correlation more than two thousand years ago.

The *Huang-di Nei-jing*, the 'bible' of Chinese medicine – written between 300 and 100 BC – lists seven emotions which can affect the health of the body: joy, anger, sadness, grief, melancholy, fear and fright. And natural medicine knows precisely which organs and processes they influence. Fear can affect the kidneys, the bladder, the genitals, the ears, the knees, the lymph system; anger acts upon the liver, the gall bladder, the muscles, the eyes; grief and melancholy influences the lungs, the large intestine, the skin, the hair, the nose, the immune system. And so on.

We may or may not make the connection to sickness, but this knowing is also part of our language, part of our lore. Take anger and the eyes: don't we say anger makes us *see* red? Or consider fear and the bladder: don't we all know some youngster who, in a moment of extreme fear, has suddenly wet his or her pants? And what about the link between grief and the lungs? My grandmother used to say 'Lungs are grief' when I had recurring bronchitis as a child. Then she'd talk about my dead mother and encourage me to cry.

'We inherit the products of the thought of other men,' wrote Ayn Rand in *The Fountainhead*. 'We inherit the wheel. We make a cart. The cart becomes an automobile. But all through the process what we receive from others is only the end product of their thinking. The moving force is the creative faculty which takes this product as material, uses it and originates the next step.'

This was exactly what Mandel did. Against the backdrop of 2,000 years of Chinese medicine, and the insights of pioneers like Paracelsus, Hahnemann and Heuss, he began to scrutinize the nature of conflict. His 'moving force' was his conviction that conflict is not only the root cause of sickness, but holds the key to its prevention as well.

Typically, he began with what he calls his 'farmer's intelligence', or common sense. He started with the obvious, with the understanding that no one lives a life free of conflict. At the same time, he kept in mind that conflict – past, present or future – does not necessarily equal sickness.

'I see life as a process of learning – and if we can learn to understand what a conflict is saying to us, then the goal has been reached and the conflict exists no longer,' he explained. 'And then the next conflict comes along so we can go on learning. This is the normal sequence of life.'

Then what of the conflicts that make us sick? 'Another word for disease-causing conflict is "conflict-stress",' he stated. 'If an athlete, for example, is in the stress of competition, adrenaline and noradrenaline, the "flight or fight" hormones, are released into the blood, and the immune system is lowered.

'The same mechanisms occur with emotional conflict. A tension, a cramp is created within the physical sphere and the immune system is weakened, just as with the athlete's stress – but the basic difference is that an unresolved emotional conflict lasts for twenty-four hours, not just for the duration of a sporting event.

'No one could exist for long under this kind of stress, and we have an inbuilt mechanism for suppressing conflict, for setting things aside because we're unable to find a solution at the moment. But this mechanism does not get rid of the conflict, it only represses it. And this suppression leaves its traces behind.

'And then we're faced with the same situation again, because it is the nature of unresolved conflict to repeat itself. It might look different, it might be in a different context, but it's always the same conflict. And we suppress it once more.

'If conflicts occur on the same level again and again, and are continually suppressed, a specific organ gets sick.'

And where do they begin, these conflicts that we suppress? Mandel's observation is that a person's rudimentary conflicts begin with conception. 'During the prenatal period the relationship between the mother and father is absorbed emotionally by the child,' he said. 'And if there are certain strains – like an attempted abortion, or anger between the parents, or some kind of poisoning from smoking or drinking – an emotional imprint will result, and it will remain with the child.

'Then there are early childhood conflicts where a child is under pressure from his father and mother, from teachers and friends. And then come the conflicts of puberty.

'In my experience, there are not hundreds of different conflicts, but only one or two or three which recur one's whole life long, always on a different level, and always with a different expression. If a person's fundamental conflict is fear, the things he fears will change as he grows. Of what he is afraid is irrelevant; the basic, underlying conflict is fear itself.'

If he wanted to prevent illness, Mandel realized, he needed a system that could help solve these hidden conflicts and, by doing so, assist his patients in stepping off the track that leads to disease.

'There were already many Colourpuncture systems that contributed to this end. We had Prenatal therapy, Father/Mother therapy and the Transmitter Relays: simple possibilities to unlock the learning potential contained in experiences which have been set aside – and, as a result, hinder the development of disease.

'The problem was that people still had not learned how to encounter future conflicts and resolve them. This meant that, after treatment, a new conflict would build up in a short time and get suppressed once again.'

He began to ponder how it could be possible to resolve old conflicts, the ones that cause disease, and, at the same time, to provide an impulse to learn from conflict, to acknowledge it when it comes, to resolve it then and there.

He knew intuitively that the solution wasn't going to be an intellectual one. 'Living contains an inbuilt learning process, but it doesn't come from the outside, from the intellect, it comes from inside the person himself or herself,' he said. 'The intellect actually creates a barrier that hides unresolved conflict, and what was needed was a system to bypass the intellect and expand people's consciousness.'

In *Vibrational Medicine*, Dr Richard Gerber wrote: 'To truly help people in distress, doctors must begin to understand that illness is partly due to a blockage within the human energy system, and especially within the individual's structure of emotional expression. This blockage can impede the flow of spirit and of the individual's higher consciousness into the conscious waking life.'

This was precisely the process Mandel set out to reverse.

'My focus was to find a possibility for changing the imprints we acquire in the womb, in childhood and in puberty, and which, in one form or another, repeat themselves our whole life long,' he stated. 'Our brain does not easily let go of conditioned programs once they've been implanted. And in later years, if a person becomes ill, he no longer has a connection to these early imprints. He actually has no idea they exist at all – yet these imprints are so strong, and so deeply ingrained, that they impede the actualization of the person's own life program. And this creates internal pressure, inner conflict.

'My impetus was the idea that if the program of a computer software system can be modified, the same must be true of the bio-informative software that controls the workings of the human brain.'

There is, in fact, a computer system modelled after the neurons in a biological nervous system and intended to simulate the way in which the brain processes information, learns and remembers. Via the introduction of 'weighted' information impulses (weak to strong or negative to positive) the interconnected processing elements that comprise the network 'learn' by association and recognition – and with adjustment, time and repetition, can be made to produce appropriate outputs. A type of artificial-intelligence system, neural networks are used in such areas as speech analysis and pattern recognition.

If, Mandel reasoned, informational input can influence a computer system (especially one that's actually *based* on the structure of the human brain itself) to recognize patterns and learn from them, then the same must be possible for man himself.

The soul-spirit colours

Mandel already had, he was to discover, the imprint-changing tools he needed – four new 'soul-spirit' colours he'd developed for stimulating the deeper levels of consciousness.

The new colours had evolved during his efforts to find a resolution to father/mother issues – the primary imprint that most influences our lives.

Egg and sperm come together, and in the shelter of the womb two aspects merge into one. Nine months later we're rudely expelled, and when we open our eyes it's on to this world of polarity – and there those two aspects are once again. Now they're called Mother and Father.

Through the mother the child learns femaleness; through the father, maleness. But these principles are taught via the will, the viewpoint, the experiential filter of the parents, and rarely consider the uniqueness of the child – despite the fact that he or she is here to live his or her own life, not to mimic or consummate theirs.

And what is it we learn about being a woman, about being a man? It all depends on the yardsticks we're given, on the home life we witness. We can grow up to see that to be female is to be loving and supportive – or, by the same token, to be cowed and subservient or angry and frustrated. And the same is true of maleness. Daddy can be a pal, a hero, a guide; he can also be a despotic terror, battering the mother, browbeating the children or abusing them sexually under the cover of night.

Reared with love or raised in fear, we all rebel in adolescence. The rebellion is against these imprints because, whether or not we're able to verbalize it, we sense in our guts that we're living borrowed lives. I remember the realization, in my early teens, that virtually nothing I said was authentically mine. My opinions and values were my father's, my stepmother's, and I fought and railed against them, burning to discover who, in truth, I really was. Others, crushed by parental power, simply give in and give up. Either way, we're all imprinted.

In traditional colour therapy, red is the colour of the father; green, of the mother. The classical zones of treatment are the navel for the mother, and the thyroid, the throat, for the father. And this is where Mandel began.

'But it was a mistake,' he recalled. 'I soon realized that if we have an overpowering mother imprint, and treat the navel area with green, we nourish the imprint, enlarging it. And the same is true with red for the father.

'So I turned it around. I said, "If I want to dislodge the mother I must call upon the father for help. And vice versa." And this became my first system for treating father/mother conflicts.'

Soon, however, he saw that more was required than just easing the burden of childhood. What was also needed was to strengthen one's own intrinsic sense of maleness and femaleness; in other words, he had to find a connection to the higher, spiritual principles of masculinity and femininity that bring harmony and cohesion to our inner and outer lives. For inspiration and guidance, Mandel turned to the research of his friend and mentor, the colour explorer Professor Gerhard Heuss.

'Heuss regarded red as the principle of Dionysus, the earthly, punishing father, and green as the principle of Kali, the mother who devours her children,' Mandel stated.

'Heuss said that these principles have to be elevated in our lives – red to crimson, to the principle of Apollo, to pure maleness, to spiritual creativity; and green to light green, to the principle of Gaia, to the spiritual mother who asks nothing in return.

'I intuitively understood that if this could happen inside a person, he would then become coherent; he would move neither towards chaos nor towards order, but would remain in the middle. And then he would be able to travel with ease on his own path.'

And so two of Mandel's four soul-spirit colours came into being: crimson and light green.

'Light green represents infinite security and peace. It is the colour of pure goodness, which seeks no reward,' he said. 'Crimson is its spiritually complementary colour, the colour of unsullied humanity, the indicator of absolute, internal "beingness" which, for me, is the purpose of this life.'

What was still missing, he told Verena and me, was a colour for a concept he described as 'the spirit core'. He needed a colour to touch the incarnated spirit, the passenger in the shuttle from birth to death. 'After extensive experiments,' he said, 'the reactions prompted by the colour rosé corresponded precisely to my notion of the spirit core.'

Equating our voyage through life with colour's own journey from primordial black to numinous white, he explained: 'The progression of life from absolute material darkness through progressive shades of grey is accompanied by colour until everything returns to pure white. Just before this happens, just before the black of matter becomes the white of pure light, there is a whiff of rosé. It is the highest manifestation of this dimension before we enter the realm of the divine. To me, rosé symbolizes a new beginning and, I was to discover, can also be helpful in finding a fresh start in life.'

The final soul-spirit colour, light turquoise, he already had.

Turquoise had always fascinated Mandel. Among the seven spectral colours it is the only one with no complementary colour. There is a red/green, blue/orange and yellow/violet relationship, but turquoise stands on its own. In his practice, he'd seen that the other colours delivered informative impulses to the body, but that turquoise had a unique capacity for touching psychological issues. He called it 'the elevator to the subconscious' and saw it as the colour of the soul.

'The soul is the middleman between body and spirit, and, as such, has a dual function,' he said. 'In an outward direction the soul exerts an influence on the body, and in an inward direction, on the spirit. After intense observation, I came to the conclusion that turquoise is the connection between these outer and inner aspects. I found dark turquoise to be the colour connection between psyche and body, and light turquoise, between psyche and spirit. Dark turquoise relates to external, physical symptoms, and light turquoise to blockages in the deep subconscious.'

The soul-spirit colours are always applied in the same sequence: light turquoise, light green, crimson and finally rosé. As I understand it, light turquoise opens the door to the depths of the subconscious; light green activates our inbuilt awareness of nature's beneficence; crimson touches the core of our being; and rosé imparts the impulse for a new beginning. Together, in combination, they flood the blockage with the regulating informative energy of absolute spirit, erasing the potential for sickness imprinted on the brain.

'All four soul-spirit colours stand for a particular love of being human; they carry in them the secret of exaltation,' Mandel summarized. 'They transfer this love, this exaltation to our beings to help us resolve structures that have become rigid. They are merely the stimulus a person needs to abandon the rut he's stuck in and set forth on an upward path.'

The way in which the soul colours work can be difficult to assimilate – and, by way of assistance, I offer this illustration.

Recently, on the inside of one arm at the elbow, I noticed a circular inflammation that spread a little more each day. And then, suddenly, a similar patch appeared on the other arm as well. Eczema, psoriasis and ringworm were among the diagnostic labels I was offered, but what troubled me most was *where* the disturbance was. In Esogetic terms, the skin is connected to the lung/large intestine function circle, and the related emotion is melancholy – and this eruption was precisely on the area Mandel calls the Zone of Grief!

But grief for what? My mother's death? My second mother's demise? Some other sorrow? Over the years I'd dealt with these emotional scars, but there were obviously still traces remaining in the body, and now they had decided to surface. The body, evidently, has its own memory.

I tried a few Colourpuncture treatments with the spectral colours, and a couple of homoeopathic remedies, but my skin refused to heal. It would improve marginally after the treatments, then worsen again. At the same time I began to notice an undercurrent of sadness, too vague to assign to any specific event. Then John Barlow, a friend and Colourpuncturist, gave me a treatment with the soul-spirit colours, irradiating the Triangle of Melancholy that Mandel had identified on the hands. It was a two-pronged attack, John told me. Treating this triangle would help resolve any lingering grief, as well as its external manifestation on my skin.

Many of us tend to process at night, during our sleep – and next morning I awoke to a feeling of lightness, to the awareness that a burden had been lifted. And when I checked my arms the skin was almost normal. There was no need, no pull to understand intellectually; I knew, intuitively, that healing had begun. I sensed it inside; I saw it on the outside. And that was enough.

Physical symptoms are our being's call for a shift in consciousness, and once the shift is made on the inside the outer symptoms disappear. The common cold offers the classic example: to the natural-health practitioner, a cold is the body's response to a 'noseful' – an inner cry for a break from the rat race, for a little dose of personal space. Perhaps this is why, from allopathic medicine, no 'cure' for the cold has ever been forthcoming. Perhaps simply getting the message non-intellectually – by inwardly understanding that we've been overdoing it, that we need to be more considerate of ourselves – is the catalyst that actually triggers the healing, the impulse that finally clears the head. As American naturalist Henry David Thoreau put it: ' 'Tis healthy to be sick sometimes.'

Mandel's soul-spirit colours work by touching deep, subconscious issues with an impulse for wholeness. And healing happens through an expansion of consciousness, at a level higher than intellect, beyond the finite mind.

Dr Kristen, who deciphered the Kirlian photos of two patients for us in an earlier chapter, told me a story that illustrates this point precisely.

A woman, Edith, came to her practice complaining of severe headaches, of attacks that lasted from two to three days at a time. And no drug helped: even the strongest sleeping pill did nothing; she always awoke to find the headache still there.

After three Colourpuncture treatments, Edith showed up for the next session looking utterly miserable. 'What's wrong?' Dr Kristen asked.

'My headache's gone,' she replied glumly.

'That's great! But why do you look so sad?'

'Because my children are going to die.'

Questions about her family's current state of health ensued, each eliciting a negative answer – until it suddenly dawned on Dr Kristen that this woman, via her concern for her children, was actually coming face to face with the inevitability of her own mortality. 'When I suggested this to her, as gently as possible, she simply couldn't answer,' Dr Kristen said. 'She crumbled, shaking and crying, in front of my eyes.'

In the following session Edith's pattern became clear. Her headaches had begun when her grandmother died, and whenever any question of death began to surface, she would develop a headache to suppress the notion, to bury it away.

'Edith has now faced the fact that she, like all of us, is going to die some day – and so there's no longer any need for the headaches,' Dr Kristen said. 'This is one of the beauties of Colourpuncture. It eliminates the physical symptoms so that the underlying issue can be addressed.'

'In Colourpuncture, we don't want to *do* anything to the person,' stated Mandel. 'If the impulse is right, the individual is going to heal himself.'

Conflict Solving therapy

Peter Mandel now turned his attention to developing the system he envisaged – one that would resolve old, suppressed conflicts, while delivering an impulse to solve new conflicts as they come along.

In his search for hints to therapeutic possibilities, Mandel carefully scrutinized whatever relevant research he could find. And as early as 1979, statements had already begun to appear in independent medical literature setting forth the very strong probability that the cause of cancer and other heavy diseases might well be emotional conflict.

'Although these ideas were extremely radical at the time, I found I was also of the same opinion – only on a different level,' he recalled. 'For example, the prevailing consensus was that, in terms of causing illness, the patient's last, or most recent conflict, is the pertinent one.

'I do not agree. I think it's a chain of unresolved conflicts which, at a certain point in time, create a final conflict – and then the barrel starts overflowing and, suddenly, the potential for disease manifests. My experience with diseases, minor to major, indicates that it is long-past events which play the most important role.'

One of the more meaningful clues which assisted him in developing the system he sought was the theory that different types of conflicts were lodged in different parts of the brain.

'I already knew that the brain works on a holographic basis, and that the pattern that vibrates in the brain is divided, physiologically, into three parts,' Mandel said. 'We have a stem brain, a midbrain or limbic system, and a cortex, and each has a different task. The stem brain is the habitual brain, the reptile brain; the midbrain is the mammal brain, the brain of emotion; and the cortex is the human brain, divided into two hemispheres to express polarity.

'In a normal, happy life, these three parts are attuned, vibrating together in harmony. If this synchronization is present, the individual does not have a great potential for repressing conflict. If this synchronization is out of kilter – as is generally the case today – the potential for suppressing conflict becomes greater and greater.

'These three parts of the brain have to be brought into accord.'

This he accomplished by locating lines on the forehead relating to the three layers of the brain. He also incorporated two triangles – the Triangle of the Subconscious on the left ear, for touching buried issues, and the Triangle of Intellect on the right ear, to stimulate understanding. And thus his Conflict Solving therapy was born.

Combined with the soul-spirit colours, it performed precisely as he expected it would. 'After some time it became clear that this system was able to activate the potential for resolving conflict,' he said. 'We found that the impulse we were giving was touching the issues in the brain, in the psyche, in the deep subconscious, and setting people on the path to resolution. The potential for sickness was being erased in the brain and, at the same time, the system was delivering an impulse for dealing with future conflict.'

To support the new therapy, he also incorporated an astrological system for regulating the expression of the life program, for harmonizing life information that had gone astray.

'Each incarnation is like a computer chip, carrying the life program of the individual – and if we accept the premise of astrology, then this program must be repeated in all systems, according to the holographic principle,' he explained. 'The astrology system shines a light on the lessons the individual is here to learn.'

He decided to include his astrology system in treating conflict because, he said, 'A disease means something in a person's life; it carries a potential for growth and for an expansion of consciousness. The name of the disease makes no difference.

'I am totally convinced that the person who uses his disease to search, to examine his life, and who, inside himself, has the feeling that there is something in this illness for him, is going to overcome it. I have seen it happen again and again. There must be a reason for spontaneous healings, and to me, the reason lies in the sudden resolution of a deep-seated conflict, in taking a jump and becoming free – not because of any divine intervention.'

As he treated patients with his Conflict Solving therapy, he found that they often complained of feeling old pains – a sure sign, to Mandel, that the conflict had been touched. For example, if a patient with cancer had undergone a gall-bladder operation, he might re-experience the pain of the colic he'd suffered before surgery. Then, when that pain was eased, he might go through a migraine or some other discomfort he'd felt even earlier.

The nature of pain is to flood the brain; there's no space for reflection or for anything else. Mandel's approach had always been to free his patients of pain as quickly as possible, and now he was able to offer relief within seconds – with a new infra-red torch used in connection with yet another topography he'd identified on the skull.

'Around 1988 I first had the idea that if, on the skin of the body, there are reflex fields that correlate to the internal organs, there must also be a similar field on the skull,' he said. 'But the idea was murky and no details came. Then suddenly one day, like a hologram, the whole skull topography appeared in a flash. It took me over half an hour to write it down.'

Everything, he found, was reproduced on the cranium – the skeleton, the organs, the senses, the function circles, the prenatal period, each and every aspect of our physiology, of the physical aspect of our lives. The topography was arranged in layers, like the skin of an onion. Peel away one layer, and another map was there.

Applied on the appropriate points on his skull topography, the infra-red tool alleviated pain in a matter of seconds, by dissolving blockages formed by interference patterns in the holographic human brain.

Interference – the phenomenon of two or more wave motions interweaving to produce an overlapping pattern – is the basis of holography.[1] It is also a property of the human brain, created by the travelling, intersecting waves of electrical and chemical impulses by which neurons transmit and process information between different parts of the body.

From the five senses, perception impulses travel to the hypothalamus, and by a process of comparison with memory and experience, new interference patterns are created – and this results in the ongoing composition of new, permanent impressions. 'This means that interference patterns are constantly developing, and doing so in permanence,' Mandel said. 'It also means that the individual is constantly creating himself anew, which quantum physicists say the universe itself also does.' (Another illustration of the cosmic law, 'As above so below'.)

According to David Bohm, this creation manifests in an outward motion, as an unfolding out of the primary or 'enfolded' level of reality where form originates. Thought is also a subtle form of matter, and this process of 'unfolding', in human terms, means that an image in the mind can eventually manifest as a reality in the physical body – precisely what the Chinese master meant by his statement, 'Disease is a thought'.

The fact that interference patterns develop 'in permanence' explains the static, frozen nature of hidden, unresolved conflict. 'There is a rigidity in ill people, and this indicates to me that they have come to a still point, where the outward motion has stopped, and with it the creative, consciousness-developing force,' Mandel added. 'It is because of this that a person gets sick.'

Mandel's infra-red torch thaws this rigidity and restores the natural interference patterns in the brain – and within ten to twenty seconds, in accordance with the holographic principle, the corresponding sectors in the body begin vibrating in the same coherent rhythm. Harmony is restored; pain is relieved.

In some cases, however, his infra-red torch didn't seem to work. And it took some time to understand why. After a period of focused investigation, he found that infra-red freed his patients of pain when the physical manifestation of the conflict was already extreme, but that it didn't work if the chain of causes was still lodged in the mental or subconscious area.

And, as usual, he discovered his solution – this time in a decorative object that had been sitting on his desk: a rose-quartz ball. It was another of his intuitive actions: he picked it up, felt its energy and gave it a try. And it worked. When infra-red, applied to appropriate points on the skull topography, did not produce immediate relief from pain, the rose quartz did.

'I envision the frequency of the rose quartz as the frequency of the heart, and I now use it to induce love into the area which no longer functions,' Mandel said. 'And it is positively amazing to see how quickly reactions come.'

'The rose-quartz frequency is usually connected to the heart chakra, and the love/wisdom ray,' I was told by Stephanie Collins of the International College of Crystal Healing in Surrey, England. 'We all know the power of love and its reputation to "conquer all". Perhaps the combination of rose quartz, for love, and the archetypal shape of the sphere, for power, releases blocks and opens doorways within the consciousness to a very pure and high level.'

The Conflict Solving system, the astrology points, the infra-red tool and the rose-quartz ball – all of these combined to form what Mandel calls 'the big pot of conflict resolution'.

'I have to say that Conflict Solving is not the panacea for everything,' he told Verena and me. 'I know that disease is always unresolved conflict, no matter if it's a cold, a cancer or a corn on the foot. I don't say that I have found a cure-all for treating cancer or other serious diseases, but I can say with total certainty that there is a possibility, through Esogetic medicine, to solve conflicts, regardless of the illness.

'At present, in my practice, between 40 and 50 per cent of the people who come with so-called incurable diseases are free of sickness or free of symptoms and leading happy, productive lives again within a quarter of a year. This is a huge number. And I am convinced that if I keep on working on this Conflict Solving model we will find out why, with certain people, their illnesses cannot be resolved.'

There are other criteria to be taken into consideration, like the individual's own life program. 'There are obviously people who have to learn through suffering, who may have to go through certain processes because of their incarnational course,' Mandel said. 'Sometimes it may be too early to treat them, because their individual process is as yet incomplete. Maybe two years down the line this process is finished and then we can treat them, then they can become free.

'There are still many questions, but, at the moment, I am very pleased that we can help people where no one else, through surgery or drugs or other therapies, has been able to succeed.'

To illustrate this, I solicited case histories from Colourpuncture therapists around the world. Verena and I were staggered by the number of success stories that poured in: from practitioners in America and Australia, Italy and Israel, Switzerland and Scandinavia, Japan and Austria, Holland and India and Brazil. And from Bruchsal and Munich, Cologne and Hamburg, from the clinics of Mandel's home territory, from Germany itself. These case histories, complete with treatments, would fill a book on their own.

Over and above the 'cures', the heart-warming reports of 'terminal' patients now free of disease, what impressed me particularly was the change in their attitudes, and the resulting turnaround in quality of life. Suddenly, people's death sentences were being commuted; all at once there was a new lease of life. Fear and rage, helplessness and resignation gave way to positivity, to optimism, to a life-affirming approach, and this, in itself, is a prime healing force. And the effects are visible, inside and out.

Franz, 71, came to the Bruchsal clinic after an operation for cancer of the colon. As well as post-operative difficulties with his bladder and prostate, he showed metastases in the liver and lungs. For three days, he underwent a program of intensive Colourpuncture treatment, including Conflict Solving therapy. After the first day of treatment, Franz lost the pale grey skin colour typical of patients with malignant tumours. Ten days later, his wife called to tell Mandel they'd just had a lab report placing his blood count within the norm. 'He's flowering visibly', was how she described the way her husband looked and how he felt.

Then there's Jim, 72, an educator and psychologist from Rosemary Dass's practice in California, suffering from angina and Parkinson's disease. After a period of initial treatment he improved noticeably, and because he was taking a business trip to Europe, Dass suggested he visit Bruchsal. There, Jim went through a three-day intensive, just like Franz, and resumed treatment with Dass when he returned to California. Today, the progress of the Parkinson's has been arrested, his tremors have decreased, his use of the control drug Sinamet has been halved, and his angina pains have ceased.

'The Conflict Solving and other treatments have helped Jim re-conceptualize the next phase of his life,' Dass said. 'When I began treating him, he was living with a tremendous sense of loss and fear: loss of his former vitality and fear that death would take him before he completed what he had come here to do in this life. He has since moved, increased his contact with people, and begun a small teaching group to pass on the insights he has gained from 20 years as a therapist.'

A similar scenario happened with a patient of Eduardo Zaba who runs a Colourpuncture clinic in Jerusalem. His client, a 48-year-old female psychologist named Yael, had a long history of cancer. First there was breast cancer and a year of chemotherapy before she was pronounced cured. Zaba, however, wasn't convinced: her Kirlian photo indicated the cancer had simply gone underground. A month later it surfaced: in the hip bone and in the joints of the lower back. He sent her to Bruchsal for five days and then continued treating her when she returned to Israel.

The Conflict Solving therapy, Zaba said, changed Yael's life. There's a new job, a new relationship, and she's finally back to living a full and normal life – without cancer.

Success with life-threatening diseases is not limited to Bruchsal; for a patient with an illness that is traditionally terminal, a visit to Mandel is not the only way to survive. With Conflict Solving and other therapies, John Barlow, for example, has helped free Louise, a 34-year-old Australian mother of two, of the debilitating symptoms of leukaemia. 'Her spleen, liver and lymphatic enlargements are virtually gone and her blood tests continue to improve,' he told me. 'And she now has a "yes" to life she's never known before.'

Manohar Croke, a Colourpuncture practitioner from Boulder, Colorado, reports the same 'yes' from Mary, 46. Having had breast cancer twice, a radical mastectomy and long periods of chemotherapy, Mary came to Croke after she'd gone into remission. She came, Croke said, 'to work on the emotional issues underlying her illness and to support her continued improvement in health'.

Because of Mary's unhappy childhood under the thumb of a hypercritical mother, Croke combined one particular session of Conflict Solving with Prenatal therapy – and this triggered in Mary what she described to Croke 'as a novel thought', that, in actual fact, she had a right to be alive.

'In the days following this treatment, Mary realized that she'd never conceptualized a notion like this before, and as a result, she began to feel more in touch with herself,' Croke reported. 'Today, she is doing really well. She has left a relationship that was unnourishing – and patterned after her destructive connection to her mother – resigned from her job as a prison counsellor and applied to a graduate school to study for a PhD in psychology. And her health, at her last check-up, continues to be fine.'

Eduardo Zaba has given the same new lease of life to Moshe, a 25-year-old Israeli building engineer who, with a history of childhood meningitis and hydrocephalus (water on the brain) from an accident at 19, suffered 24-hour-a-day migraines for over five years. After five treatments, primarily with Conflict Solving, the migraines stopped completely.

And what were the conflicts? I half expected, when I began perusing the case histories, to find a distinct relation between a specific conflict and a particular disease. But life's not that simple. Did Jim get Parkinson's because he had to suppress his fear of death as a runner carrying dispatches between the trenches in World War I? Or was it because he lost a testicle in a hernia operation at age six? And did Yael get breast cancer because her family sent her, a three-year-old Jewish girl, to be educated in a strict Christian monastery until she was 18? Or was it because, when she came home for a visit, her older brothers threatened to pee on her while she slept? And did Mary develop her breast cancer because her mother constantly criticized her for maturing early and having overly large breasts? And in Louise's case, was it her childhood pattern of getting sick to attract love? Or in Moshe's, was it the death, during military service, of the brother he loved?

I found myself asking if, in fact, the name of the conflict really matters. We're all individuals, all unique, and one man's dream may be another man's nightmare. I remember a woman, Rose, who'd been a severe anorexic. Years later, she told me it was because of her frizzy hair. Her mother was a ballet teacher and Rose could never tame her unruly mane into ballet's classic, slicked-back bun. And then I had another friend, Jane, with a mountain of hair as uncooperative and wiry as a ball of steel wool. She gloried in it; it was her pride and joy.

Unresolved conflict is the only issue. And whatever the conflict, it's the patient's own. Acceptance is an act of consciousness, and the first step in the healing process. There's really no role for the analytical mind.

I have a friend, Paul, who got this immediately. Recently diagnosed with one of our newest degenerative diseases, Hepatitis C, Paul turned to Colourpuncture – after no relief from allopathic medicine, and feeling even sicker from the drugs. 'My mind tries to tell me that all this light and colour is nothing but hooey,' he said to me after his second treatment, 'but I can't deny how much better I feel.' On the road to healing, it's the best encouragement there is.

The same is true of unburdening. 'Japanese people are taught to hide emotional problems, and they carry deep sorrow in their hearts,' Dr Takeshi Numakawa of Yokohama wrote to me. 'After the higher Colourpuncture treatments, people are unable to stop their tears.' Due to the freeing effect of this emotional unloading, he reports he is able to achieve 'almost one hundred per cent positive results' in the treatment of such psychological disorders as neurosis, depression, schizophrenia, chronic fatigue and general malaise.

Angelika Hochadel, a Colourpuncturist currently shifting from Germany to England, reports similar successes in treating physical manifestations – such as bulimia, visual and hearing difficulties and skin afflictions – that she and her patients were able to trace directly to unresolved childhood conflicts with mother and/or with dad.

Homework (which we'll examine in the next chapter) plays a significant role in helping people resolve these old emotional issues and open a new chapter in their lives. By doing simple, supportive treatments at home – on themselves or with the help of a family member – patients enter into a partnership with the doctor, naturopath or Colourpuncturist, working together to uproot the disease. And the benefits can be immense.

At his practice in Munich, Markus Wunderlich, Peter Mandel's son, assigns homework extensively. He teaches a family member to do Conflict Solving and other therapies at home, between sessions at the clinic.

In eight-year-old Laura's case, her mother gave the treatments. Beginning with tuberculosis of the lymph nodes at 18 months, subsequent bouts of tonsillitis, years of antibiotics and a recent operation, Laura was fragile and withdrawn when she came to Wunderlich. Within a year the child was free of tonsillitis and free of infection, and today her mother reports that Laura's more balanced and open to the people in her life.

Treatments for Fritz, 51, were administered by his wife. He was first diagnosed with cancer, with Hodgkin's lymphoma, in 1990, and underwent chemotherapy and radiation, with heavy side effects. In 1993 he came to Wunderlich for treatment. His latest examination, in April 1995, at Munich's Grosshadern clinic, showed no more cancer in his lymph system. 'Fritz is very positive, and feels very productive again,' Wunderlich said. 'He also says, because of his experience with Hodgkin's, he has changed many things in his life.'

This statement – that patients have 'changed many things' in their lives – crops up again and again in reports from Colourpuncture therapists who work with Conflict Solving therapy. People step out of repressive relationships, quit unfulfilling jobs, stand up to those who intimidate them, and give themselves permission to be who they really are. Invariably, this results in a new sense of health and well-being, and in the majority of cases, a whole new quality of life.

As Conflict Solving clears the channels of consciousness for healing to happen, it also creates space for an understanding of why we get sick. When we start to see, no matter how tentatively, that disease is a thought, that self-destructive ideas and patterns and feelings can actually make us ill, we begin to take stock, to think about prevention, to initiate change. And people who have been taken to the brink by a disease like cancer, and rescued by resolving past conflict in their lives, cannot help but view conflict in a brand new light. And just as Mandel intended when he developed the system, a significant aspect of this new focus is accepting the challenge, day by day, of dealing with any new conflict as it comes along.

8

Partners in healing

The unexamined life is not worth living.
SOCRATES

In *The Man Who Mistook His Wife for a Hat*, Dr Oliver Sacks tells the wonderful story of 93-year-old Mr MacGregor, afflicted with Parkinson's disease. Like many with Parkinson's, MacGregor walked with a noticeable tilt but was completely unaware of it. Worried he might fall and injure himself, the other residents of the old people's home commented on it regularly, saying that he reminded them of the Leaning Tower of Pisa whenever he moved about. But MacGregor stubbornly insisted he was walking just fine. And it wasn't until Sacks made a video of him in motion, and he saw himself listing a good 20 degrees to the left, that he realized his friends were telling the truth.

'The old man suddenly became intent, his brows knitted, his lips pursed,' Sacks wrote. 'He stood motionless, in deep thought, presenting the picture that I love to see: a patient in the actual moment of discovery – half appalled, half amused – seeing for the first time exactly what is wrong and, in the same moment, exactly what there is to be done. This *is* the therapeutic moment.'

It is also the moment of decision, where the patient either picks up the ball and runs with it or tosses it back into the doctor's court. And old Mr MacGregor rose to the occasion. A carpenter before retiring, he decided to build a spirit level into the rim of his spectacles – because, by his terms of reference, the Parkinson's had 'knocked out' the spirit level of balance in his brain. With the help of Sacks and an optometrist, MacGregor reconstructed his glasses, and from then on, with an eye on the gauge, he was able to check, whenever he walked, whether he was manoeuvring vertically or not – and adjust himself accordingly.

What Sacks calls 'the therapeutic moment' is the turning point in the process of healing. In this moment the patient becomes proactive, begins to work *with* the doctor or therapist to heal himself – or, as in Mr MacGregor's case, to better his quality of life.

To me, the story of old Mr MacGregor is an inspiration to anyone who's sick. He accepted the challenge of his illness and did something about it. He made his affliction less debilitating and, at the same time, took a positive step in preventing the very real possibility, with a degenerative disease like Parkinson's, of falling and hitting his head or breaking a 93-year-old bone.

I often think of Mr MacGregor and Sacks, addressing the old man's problem together in the workshop of the home. I can taste the excitement, the thrill of adventure and, after days of trial and error, the sweetness of success. And this same voyage of discovery, this journey of prevention and healing, is available to anyone who suffers – whether it's from a life-threatening disease, a chronic pain or an occasional ache.

According to Mandel, a physical symptom is the body's way of telling us that something in our lives is amiss, that somewhere there is discord and that, to be healthy, harmony has to be restored. Add to this his understanding of unresolved emotional conflict as the root cause of sickness, and we have the ingredients of a great adventure, of a pilgrimage into our own interior – where, with patience and understanding, we can uncover why we feel unhealthy, or if a symptom has already manifest, why we are sick. And herein lies the key to prevention as well.

I'm not suggesting introspection is easy or comfortable. We discover hurts others have inflicted upon us, and hurts we've inflicted upon ourselves. We see where we've been programmed to submit instead of question, to believe instead of experience, to deny our own authenticity instead of standing up for ourselves. And this process is invaluable. I see it with Verena and I see it with me. Whenever she has trouble with her body or is confronted by a situation that wounds her, she says, 'It's obviously time for one more walk in my little hurt garden,' and turns her attention inward. And I watch her, each and every time, come out of her 'little hurt garden' cleaner, clearer, and another step closer to becoming whole.

And where are the signposts, the indicators that show us the way in, the route to the root cause of our discomfort or of our disease? Esogetic medicine abounds in these pointers, and among the most helpful are the organ circuits of Dr Jochen Gleditsch, the function circles Colourpuncture uses in diagnosis and treatment. In terms of both healing and prevention, they are a treasure chest of clues.

A small example: a couple of years ago, when Verena was working as a physiotherapist in Switzerland, the wife of a local farmer came to the clinic with a painful and incapacitating bursitis of the elbow.

A bursitis is an inflammation of a bursa, a sac of fibrous, friction-reducing tissue sandwiched between tendons or ligaments and underlying bone. In function-circle methodology, elbows fall under the sway of the liver/gall-bladder organ circuit, and the emotional aspect is anger, directed outwardly or inwardly, at others or at oneself. The antidote is flexibility and tolerance, especially for one's own needs.

There is often a symbolism to symptoms that can help the therapist deduce what's going on. But only to a certain degree. Rounded shoulders may reveal that a person is feeling burdened, or a stomach ache that someone is stressed – but these clues simply guide the therapist in formulating and asking the right questions. There is no answer inherent in the symptom itself. The language of symptoms is utterly individual, and only the patient can deliver the answer which contains the cure. As in the case of the swollen elbow that troubled the farmer's wife. Only by Verena's talking to the woman, listening to her, and assessing her responses were they able, together, to identify the cause.

'From our conversation during the consultation, it became very obvious that this woman badly needed some elbow room,' Verena said. 'What with the husband and the children and the cows and the fields, she had no space for herself. So, as I worked on her elbow, I suggested she take at least five minutes a day, close the door, and say to herself, "This time is for *me*!" '

Initially, Verena reported, the farmer's wife was extremely resistant to the idea of taking time for herself. She believed it was sinful to put herself first, that the well-being of her family and the farm animals was more important than her own. Each time she came to the practice Verena would ask if she were taking her five minutes. The answer was invariably evasive, but always amounted to 'no'.

A week or so after her final physiotherapy treatment, we were shopping at the local supermarket when a woman ran up to Verena, waving her arm in the air. They spoke for a moment in Swiss German and afterwards Verena translated. 'She said she's now taking ten minutes for herself every day, and she wanted me to know that the bursitis is gone and her elbow is fine.'

By this little act, by taking a few moments for herself each day, this woman activated the greatest healing force that exists within us – the power of self-love. And the first step on the road to self-love is to assume responsibility for one's own life, sick as well as fit.

These days, the notion of accepting responsibility for our health is very much in vogue. Doctors, naturopaths and nutritionists advise us to eat balanced meals, take vitamin supplements, stop smoking and exercise regularly. But where sickness is concerned, 'responsibility' is still a heavily loaded word. To be told 'You are responsible for your sickness' – directly or indirectly – can be a difficult pill to swallow. It can engender feelings of guilt and shame; it can reinforce an already entrenched sense of unworthiness, because we have been raised to misunderstand what 'responsibility' actually means.

'Responsibility' has become a synonym for 'burden'. Day in, day out, we have to be responsible: for our children, for our partners, for our jobs. We live, in fact, for other people. We assume the mantle of responsibility out of guilt, out of notions of sacrifice, duty and service – and in doing so, unless we are careful, we can invalidate our own life-energy, the most precious gift we have.

What 'responsibility' truly means is *response-ability*, the ability to respond, not react, to whatever happens in our lives. When Verena's patient understood what her swollen elbow was saying, she eventually responded. Instead of blaming her husband or the farm, she gave herself the 'elbow room' her bursitis was telling her she needed. And this is precisely what 'taking responsibility' means.

There's a message in every sickness, slight or severe. And the function circles can help us decipher what our aches and pains and illnesses are trying to say.

At the same time, the function circles can play a much deeper role in bringing harmony and wholeness to our lives, by helping us identify and clarify the life lessons we have come here to learn. And this is as true for those who see themselves as basically healthy, as it is for those who are physically sick. As long as we are embodied in this dimension, functioning in polarity, there are issues to be resolved and lessons to be learned. And like it or not, we learn through suffering. It's an integral part of the human condition; it's one of the fundamental ways life helps us grow.

Suffering, of course, is relative, individual. To evolve, to fulfil his unique potential, one man may require the suffering of cancer; for another, the suffering of feeling inadequate may be enough. The challenge, the adventure, is recognizing where our suffering is rooted, in which aspect of our lives. Then, and only then, can we sweep clean our private path to wholeness, with all the blessings this image implies.

The real significance of suffering – as it is with responsibility – is widely misunderstood. Generation after generation, we have been conditioned to believe that the causes of our suffering lie outside ourselves. And it's simply not true. Consider an issue as commonplace as stress. These days, more and more medical practitioners are beginning to acknowledge that many illnesses – ulcers, heart attacks, skin afflictions, even certain cancers – are stress-related, and that stress is a direct by-product of lifestyle. Now, if *we* are not responsible for how we live our lives – and the resulting psychological and physical suffering – then who is?

The switch in attitude came for me with the recognition that suffering is not necessarily negative, but also includes a positive side. The catalyst was a statement of Gautam Buddha: 'Growth is a by-product of suffering.' At first, this shook me profoundly, yet the more I pondered the Buddha's observation, the more I became convinced of its undeniable truth. Looking back over my own life, at my growth milestones, I see that each time we take another step up life's ladder, it is because we resolve some block, childhood or otherwise, from which we've been suffering. And where suffering had once hindered our evolution, it suddenly becomes an opportunity for growth. It's all a question of attitude.

Let's move again into the function circles, and look at the hints to healing and prevention they contain.

As outlined in earlier chapters, there are five, distinct function circles or organ circuits: kidney/bladder, liver/gall-bladder, lung/large intestine, spleen-pancreas/stomach and heart/small intestine. Mandel likens each to a big drawer. Inside each are organs and emotions, body parts and processes, life lessons to learn and issues to resolve.

Movement is a law of life, and this applies to these organ circuits as well. Man or woman, we're all born into the kidney/bladder function circle, and from here our voyage begins. We travel through these function circles repeatedly, one after another, in sequence and in an upward spiral, as we journey through life. And for the great majority of us, if we pay close attention, we'll see that there is one function circle where we continually stumble, like a ditch we fall into again and again. Travelling up the spiral, we pass through the same issues, always at a different level and from a different perspective, but the underlying disturbance is invariably the same.

Consider the fear of being alone. As a child the fear is of being left alone by the mother; as an adult, the same fear is projected on to one's lover. The object of the fear has changed with the years; the fundamental phobia hasn't.

As we move through the function circles, we may find ourselves identifying with more than one circuit, but it's easiest to start where we resonate most. This is the function circle to examine, the drawer to dig into, because here are stored the obstacles that stand in our way. Whatever the clue, focus on it: examine it inside and outside, this way and that, and its secrets will be revealed.

Before we begin this quest into our interior, however, there's one more bit of background I should like to provide. Represented in each function circle – except for the heart/small intestine – is a basic energy orientation: two have a female vibration, the other two, male. It can be a helpful consideration, because for Colourpuncture, as well as for Chinese medicine, sickness is a disturbance in our female–male polarity, in receptive/active, in the harmonious balance of yin and yang.

The female-oriented function circles are kidney/bladder and lung/large intestine; the male circuits, liver/gall-bladder and spleen-pancreas/stomach.

Imagine a pyramid (figure 8). At the first corner, place the kidney/bladder function circle; directly opposite, lung/large intestine. At the second corner, place liver/gall-bladder, and opposite, spleen-pancreas/stomach. At the centre, where the male axis meets the female axis, lies the function circle of the heart. Because of the heart's special status – which we'll examine later – it sits at the top of the pyramid, elevated above the rest. The heart is only affected when issues in the other circles remain unresolved. In terms of self-examination and self-transformation, the first four circles are where the action is.

The first 'feminine' function circle, kidney/bladder, rules the kidneys, bladder, lymphatic system, genitals, ovaries, bones, knees and the four front teeth, upper and lower. The external organ is the ear. The basic function is sensing; the emotional symptom, fear.

As well as physical problems in any of the above organs, systems, teeth or structural parts – such as a bladder infection or toothache or a lymphatic upset like fever or flu – there are other disturbances

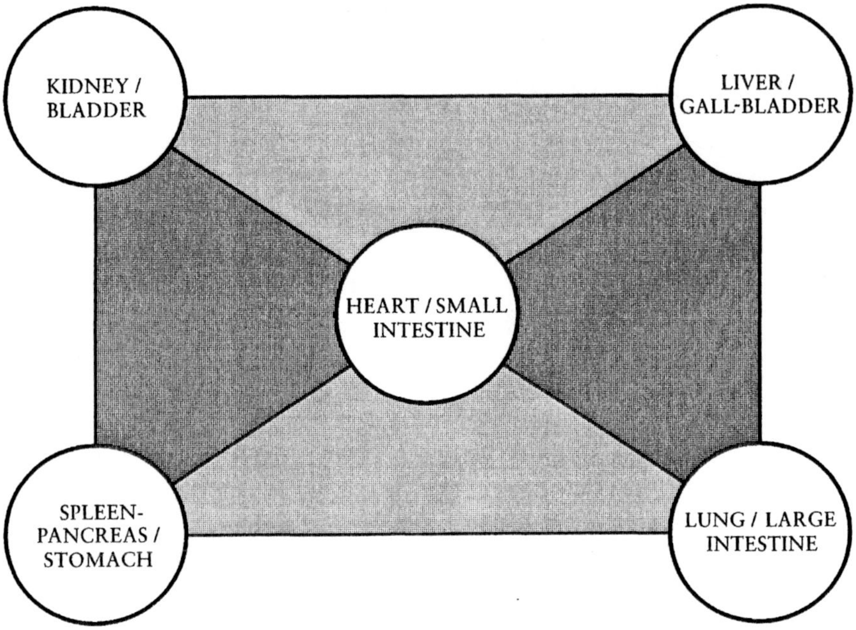

Figure 8 Pyramid plan of function circle relationship

to watch for, psychogenic indications that the kidney/bladder organ circuit is out of balance. This can be a difficulty in accepting what's happening at the moment, or an inability to listen to one's own inner voice, to heed one's own inner law. Fear, the emotional expression, is invariably existential, and projected on to some external factor, like anxiety about money or insecurity about one's partner's affections.

The potential of this organ circuit – what one can expect when it's functioning harmoniously – is a deep-seated contact with one's own inner strength and the courage to stand behind one's own convictions. This means welcoming what the moment brings, being receptive to the winds of change.

Dr Fausto Pagnamenta, the Locarno paediatrician, told me a story that offers a classic illustration of an imbalance in this organ circuit. Annually, at the beginning of the Swiss school year, his practice is flooded with first-graders suffering from infections of the ear. And this isn't his experience alone, he said. With other paediatricians it also happens, each and every year.

'The medical establishment's rationale for these ear infections is that these children, going to school for the first time, are being exposed to viruses to which they have no resistance,' he explained. 'In Mandel's view, as well as mine, these infections have nothing to do with viruses: they are the result of an emotional conflict triggered by fear. For many youngsters, a new and strange environment can be a very scary experience, especially coupled with the unfamiliar pressures of learning to read and write and calculate sums.'

He treats these children with Colourpuncture, focusing on the kidney/bladder function circle – and in four short and painless sessions, the ear infections always clear.

'Children naturally tend to be innocent and open, and they respond very quickly to colour,' he said. 'And to forestall any recurrence of infection, in the ear or elsewhere in the organ circuit, I make sure parents understand that the cause is not some virus, but an external expression of the child's inner fears. This parental understanding can make all the difference to a child's well-being, not only in the first year of school, but his or her whole life long.'

How our childhood environment can affect our adult lives is illustrated in a case history from Western Australia reflexologist and Colourpuncturist Lyn White. She told me the story of Nora, a 19-year-old Perth dancer who came to her as a last resort because of intense pain in her knee. Nora was no longer able to dance, and the doctors were suggesting surgery. White was able to relieve the pain in one session.

'When I worked with Nora I was just beginning to practise Colourpuncture and did not make the connection to the kidney/bladder function circle,' White said. 'Later, the link became very clear to both of us. Nora is a sensitive, only child, and has led a very sheltered life – and her mother, who worries excessively, has instilled a great number of fears in her daughter. Over the four years since Nora has been coming to me, we've spent a considerable amount of time talking about these fears and working together to help her overcome them.

'And she's doing wonderfully well. She is still dancing, and her knee has never troubled her again.'

The next function circle is liver/gall-bladder, the one which plagued the woman Verena treated, the farmer's wife who needed elbow room.

The basic function of this 'male' organ circuit is feeling; the emotional valve is anger or rage.

Liver/gall-bladder governs the liver, the gall bladder, the muscles and sinews, and the canine teeth. The related sensory organ is the eye – not only in the sense of seeing, registering and decoding outside images, but in terms of acknowledging what we observe within ourselves.

'In this day and age, with material ambitions dominating our lives, we are an embattled species striving to get to the top at all costs, and relaxation is rare,' Mandel observed. 'The price for all this will be felt in the liver/gall-bladder organ circuit. Anger and rage, directed at oneself or at someone else, is the outcome of the ever-increasing stress nourished by our desire for more and greater goodies.'

Not being in contact with our feelings and not expressing our energy are indications this function circle is disturbed. Consequences range from tension and contraction, frustration and aggression, to depression, lethargy and compulsiveness – whether this manifests as overeating, comfort shopping or an over-abundance of anger or stress.

People whose liver/gall-bladder organ circuit is functioning harmoniously are active and dynamic, tolerant and flexible – and all of this from a relaxed inner space.

The third function circle is lung/large intestine – and here Mandel's sequence differs from that of both Chinese medicine and Dr Gleditsch. 'In classical literature, the spleen-pancreas/stomach function circle comes before lung/large intestine,' Mandel explained. 'But because of the significance of the opposing male–female axis, I found this illogical – and that's why I changed its position.'

Lung/large intestine is the ditch I've kept falling into most of my life. Female in orientation, with intuiting as its basic function, this organ circuit rules the lungs, large intestine, the premolars (teeth four and five, counting from the central incisor), the skin, the hair and the immune system. The external organ is the nose – in terms of picking up outside aromas such as perfume, or inner, intuitive scents, like detecting a whiff of danger or 'smelling a rat'.

A lung/large intestine disturbance can manifest as holding on, resisting change, feeling shy and unworthy, or feeling guilty about whatever is going on. Melancholy, acute grief and heartache are common when this organ circuit is out of equilibrium.

The positive aspects of lung/large intestine are being intuitive, inspired and receptive to life – and this is mirrored in the way in which the lungs and large intestine operate, in their separate yet similar duties of taking in, transforming and then letting go.

In countless ways, both complex and commonplace, these function circles exert their influence on our day-to-day lives. For example, the hair is governed by lung/large intestine, and so is how we deal with things when we're standing at the threshold of something new. Now, don't we invariably get our hair cut or restyled when faced with a new situation – whether it's a first date or an interview for a new job?

The fourth function circle is spleen-pancreas/stomach. Its basic function is thinking; its vibration is male. The spleen, stomach, pancreas, joints and throat belong to this circuit, as well as the two molar teeth. The sensory key is the mouth and the lips, in terms of touching, tasting, chewing and swallowing; in other words, in terms of ingesting, for better or worse, whatever comes from the outside.

People with an imbalance in this organ circuit tend to escape their feelings by fleeing into the mind. They can be analytical, dismissively judgemental, prone to worry and obsessiveness – and stress is the inescapable result.

The stomach, as explained in an earlier chapter, has only one response to stress: acidity. And excess acidity can affect the stomach, causing ulcers, or produce arthritis by settling in the joints.

When this organ circuit is in balance, we're able to reflect and assimilate, discern without judging, and grow through our relationships with others and with the outside world.

The remedy for disorders in spleen-pancreas/stomach is meditation, the polar opposite of thinking. And this is why, in increasing numbers around the world, people are turning to meditation as the antidote to stress.

The final organ circuit, heart/small intestine, holds a special place within the five function circles. 'Beyond anything psychological, it represents our spiritual aspect and corresponds to joy, enthusiasm, sympathy and the warmth of the human heart,' Mandel explained. 'In its spiritual aspect, this organ circuit is perfect and unchangeable.'

Sprightliness, charisma and individuality are expressions of this organ pattern. Physically, it is connected to the blood, to the circulatory system, and to the wisdom teeth. The tongue, the organ of speech, is the sensory key. 'Through language,' observed Mandel, 'the person expresses himself and makes himself known for who he is.'

Disturbances in this function circle are always on a physical level, and the causes of any irregularities must always be traced to disorders in the other four organ circuits.

Examining ourselves through the lens of the function circles can provide important hints for preventing illness and bettering the quality of our lives – but in terms of remedial action, if an organ circuit is disturbed, a visit to a professional Colourpuncturist could well be the next step.

Not only can Mandel's Kirlian diagnostic system, his EEA, accurately identify the function circle that's out of kilter, it allows the therapist to pinpoint precisely where the disturbance lies – and treat it.

Get ready for homework

In a Colourpuncture session, all that's required from the patient – apart from responding to inquiries about point sensitivity and providing feedback during treatment – is to lie back, turn in and savour the light. But be prepared for homework as well. Because actively involving people in their own healing process is a fundamental precept of Esogetic medicine.

'Self-treatment has a very high priority in Colourpuncture,' said Mandel. 'Over the years, I have observed that people who treat themselves, following our instructions, experience a much faster and enduring recovery than those who hang about the offices of doctors, therapists or naturopaths.

'Only one person can heal, and that is the patient himself. In my entire life I have never healed anyone, because nobody can do that. I am only the crane that picks up the car from the ditch and sets it back on its wheels. I may be able to remove one dent or another so that the wheels can turn again, but the patient himself has to drive.

'I can support him in this. I can give him tools and treatments to do at home, to help him experience that his sickness is his and his alone.

'That's why he has to treat himself, to touch himself, to look at himself in the mirror, maybe to smile at himself and, especially, to start loving himself. A person who is sick cannot love himself.'

Nor, according to Mandel, can he trust himself.

'People trust many things,' he said. 'They trust the politicians, the priests, the parents; the only person they don't trust is themselves. This is how we have been educated: to give ourselves away.

'But what does this mean, to place our trust in others? It means we are trusting someone else's opinion, someone else's belief system, some idea the other person has created within himself. We don't need to do that; we can create our own lives. That's why Colourpuncture works to get rid of the influence of the father, of the mother, of all these imprints that belittle us, that tell us, "This is not allowed. You should be different. You must do this; you must do that." '

In the Bruchsal clinic, and those of Colourpuncturists all over the world, Mandel's directive is clear: in Esogetic medicine, it is the patient's 'absolute duty' to treat himself.

This direct involvement of the sufferer in his own healing process represents a significant departure from the traditional doctor-patient scenario. 'In orthodox medicine, the person says, "I am sick and that's what the doctor is there for", ' Mandel observed. 'So he goes to the doctor and says, "You are the doctor. Now you are responsible; I put myself in your hands. Now this sickness has nothing to do with me."

'This is utterly foolish,' he added emphatically. 'Illness is a completely individual affair. Thousands of people may have a tumour, but the tumour of Mr Smith is not the tumour of Mr Jones. Everyone's tumour is his own. Mr Smith's tumour has developed and grown inside him, so the cause has to lie within him as well. And there, inside himself, is where Mr Smith will also find the cure.'

Mandel, however, is against 'uncontrolled self-experimentation' with colour. For those who are ill, self-treatment is prescribed by trained therapists only, with the at-home treatments carefully demonstrated and explained in advance.

Personally, I enjoy treating myself immensely. I find homework like a simple coordination treatment – ten minutes in the morning – sets me up for an harmonious and productive working day.

Colourpuncture homework, however, means access to a Colourpuncture set, and most practitioners rent them at a nominal fee. And in response to the growing interest in self-help, Mandel has developed a new set, with a flat colour-light applicator instead of a pyramid focus, available at about half the price of the precision set professional Colourpuncture therapists use.

This new 'Colourzone' lamp was launched to coincide with the publication of the initial volume of Mandel's first manual of self-treatment, *Colours: The Pharmacy of Light.* Written in collaboration with his Bruchsal colleague, Andreas Pflegler, the book details basic do-at-home treatments, with illustrations to help, for a wide variety of common ailments – gastrointestinal complaints, children's illnesses, immunological imbalances and skin afflictions. Also included are cosmetic Colourpuncture treatments for combating wrinkles and ageing skin.

The second volume in the series – unpublished at time of writing – will cover heart and circulation problems, headaches and migraines, bone and joint diseases, and a number of psychological disorders.

Another homework assignment can be listening to cassettes based on Esogetic models and Colourpuncture systems transposed into sound.

The key for transposing colour into sound was discovered by Mandel and, compared to standard mathematical formulae, is completely new. Working with Mandel and using this formula, composers and musical educators Ludovika Helm and Kay Korten were able to create sequences of sounds corresponding precisely to the respective colour frequencies of each therapeutic system. In the 'Coloursound' repertoire are the Conflict Solving therapy, as well as tapes for concentration, insomnia, back pain, headaches and migraine; for motivation and spirit-body-soul wholeness; for strengthening the immune system and for psychosomatic balancing in times of stress.

'Through the ears, harmonies and rhythms directly influence the brain and the subconscious,' Mandel wrote in *Colours: The Pharmacy of Light.* 'Extensive research has shown that the brain perceives certain sound frequencies as information and passes this information on to the coordination systems. In other words, when provided with the right kind of information, the brain is able to detect and repair malfunctions.'

With the assistance of Helm and Korten, Mandel also produced a series of nine Esogetic Sound Patterns. These are exact sequences and combinations of sounds – based on his Esogetic Model – representing the interconnections between the physical body and the conscious and subconscious realms.

The Esogetic Sound Patterns mainly influence the psyche where, in Mandel's view, the root causes of many illnesses lie. They cover such issues as balance, harmony, regeneration and vitality, and support such processes as knowing oneself, attaining one's goal in life and activating the power of self-esteem.

But, without a doubt, the most widely known and most widely used of Mandel's homework products is his powerful and enigmatic Esogetic Wild Herb Oil. Used for soothing foot and body baths, or for massaging reflex zones on the skin, the Esogetic oil – as odd as it sounds – has the capacity to induce dreams.

Some 15 years ago, Mandel began to notice, first in himself and then in his patients, a relationship between particular ailments and certain types of dreams. 'Both dreams and illness are signals from the patient's subconscious to his conscious state,' he said. 'So I concluded that if I treat the area on the body connected to the ailment, it must then produce a message-giving dream.'

Over the years, through continuing observation, he was able to identify 56 zones on the body (another multiple of seven) that can be stimulated to activate specific types of dreams. From further experimentation, he discovered that application of coloured light and the 22 wild herbal essences that comprise his Esogetic oil produced precisely the dreaming impulse he'd been looking for.

Many of our dreams are insignificant, nothing more than our subconscious tossing out the unnecessary rubbish we accumulate during our waking day. But others have deeper implications, and can often provide very valuable hints to our mental and physical welfare.

With Mandel's system, dreamwork includes keeping notes. 'I explain to people that they are going to dream more and recommend that they keep a dream diary,' he said. 'I tell them to jot down the dreams they remember, but not to read the diary for two or three weeks. At that point they will suddenly see a thread running through their dreams, and they will have their own insights as to the meaning and direction in which their dreams are pointing.

'Focusing too much on the symbols that have been written about in dream literature can implant ideas in people's minds. This is disrespectful; I don't want to do that. What I am looking for is the dreams of the individual and the clues they contain. One man's dreams are saying something to him and to him alone.

'Dreaming can be a great support to the healing process, because in dreams the subconscious is trying to tell us something.

'And if we can learn to listen to ourselves with love and trust – to the messages of our dreams and the clues contained in the function circles – then perhaps there will be no reason for illness, no more need to get sick.'

9

A tool for consciousness

Real healing has to do with the removal of all that stands between us and the truth.
RESHAD FEILD
The Invisible Way

Colourpuncture, states Peter Mandel, cures by freeing the consciousness in the cells. When I first considered this statement I had no difficulty understanding it intellectually – because of his solid esoteric and energetic foundation, his decades of clinical proof. Today, however, that understanding has penetrated far deeper. No longer is it simply a function of intellect; I now know from my own experience that what he says is true.

Way down inside myself, in the very energy fabric of my organism, it feels as if a spotlight has gone on. There's a consciousness, an awareness in my body and of my body that's never been so pronounced. There were times when the occasional message would come through – like enough tomatoes or eggs for a while – but never as clearly, or consistently. I now feel freshly tuned to my body's natural wisdom – with a new awareness of what it needs and what it doesn't need, of what it requires to be harmonious, of how to support it in becoming and remaining whole.

This process of consciousness is strange and mysterious: it's a hearing with an inner ear, a sensing with an inner nose, a seeing with an inner eye. And the master of these inner senses is the greatest mystery of all. This is not the 'I' of ego or of personality, this is the witnessing consciousness, the transcendental 'I' of being – because, in actual fact, this is who we truly are. In our essence we're neither Verenas nor Jacks nor Peter Mandels; we're each a ray of the universal consciousness, a silent presence perched alongside the river of being, watching the waves and currents of life flowing by.

Meditators know the workings of consciousness well. In activity or in inactivity, there's a constant witnessing – of the mind and emotions, of the entire play of existence, inside and out. And it's the most freeing thing there is. Slowly but surely, by witnessing, by shining the light of awareness on our inner world, we become the master in our own house. We can choose to get caught up in the mind or swamped by emotion; we can let thoughts and feelings arise, decide to become engaged or just allow them to go. It's all up to us. It's our choice to be happy or unhappy, burdened or unburdened, loving or unloving, healthy or sick. Once the witnessing consciousness is activated there's no more passing the buck.

Unlike thousands of others, I didn't come to Colourpuncture via a major illness or even a minor physical complaint. Existence has its own timing; we get what we need when the moment is ripe. Colourpuncture appeared in my life when I needed a light in the darkness, a focus on the imprints of early childhood and the prenatal time. Those once inaccessible events are now out in the open, and the patterns they set in motion, the conflicts they initiated, have been resolved. As Mandel puts it, there's been a freeing, an expansion of consciousness – and I feel the effect across the totality of my being: spirit and emotion, body and mind.

The same thing, he says, happens to those who have never given a thought to meditation in their lives. As Colourpuncture helps them cure their ills, and they begin to experience a new physical and emotional harmony, many people report a sudden interest in spirituality, in meditation, in wanting to explore the higher dimensions of existence, and of themselves.

This is why I call Colourpuncture a tool for consciousness. By freeing the consciousness in the cells, an upward flow is set in motion – from below to above – and a light begins to permeate one's being. A flame is kindled, an urge to travel the path to even greater consciousness, to even greater wholeness – and meditation is the door.

'The words "medicine" and "meditation" come from the same root,' said Osho in *Walking in Zen, Sitting in Zen*. 'Meditation is the ultimate medicine: it cures you of all ills.'

And why? Because meditation takes us to the unpolluted oneness of the source, to that silent space of inner beingness beyond the outer dramas of the body, of the emotions, of the mind. And slowly, with practice, this connection to the wellspring becomes moment-to-moment, an ongoing affair. Whatever we're doing, wherever we are, there's a remembering of where we've come from, of the benediction of who we are.

As growth is a by-product of suffering, witnessing is a by-product of meditation. And by experiencing who we truly are – the witnessing consciousness – it becomes increasingly apparent who we are not. And when we acknowledge the obstacles blocking our path to health and wholeness – the imprints, the shocks and traumas; the shoulds and shouldn'ts, the dos and don'ts – we can take positive steps to resolve them, to sweep them away.

Or we can start from the other direction. Like my friend Louise.

As head of communications at the Sydney branch of a multinational investment house, Louise was suffering from a classic case of executive stress. Long hours, plus regular jaunts to New York one week and Singapore the next, were taking their toll, and the company offered a week of rest and recuperation at the health farm of her choice.

In addition to diet and physical exercise, the spa she selected offered programs for growth. And one of them triggered a dramatic turnaround in Louise's attitude to herself and the way she was living her life.

'Every 15 minutes, over a two-day period, we had to write down who we were at that given moment,' she told me. 'By the afternoon of the first day, I realized that I hadn't a clue who I was. I found myself writing what I thought about myself, or what I felt about myself, but nothing about who I am. I was writing *opinions*, and a lot of them belonged to other people; they weren't even mine!

'It was a real shock, seeing that I didn't know myself at all,' she said. 'So I started to meditate. And it's changing my life.'

The night-time constellations may be upside down, and Christmas may come on a hot summer's day, but living in Australia is not so different from being in England or America or anywhere else.

Our book stores are also filled with books on meditation: by doctors like Deepak Chopra, Bernie Siegel and Dean Ornish, documenting the success of meditation in treating cancer, HIV or heart disease; and by meditators writing how-to guidebooks for those who want to feel healthier, to improve the quality of their lives.

People from all walks of life are gravitating towards meditation. Some are doing Chinese *t'ai chi* or Indian yoga; Buddha's Vipassana, Osho's Dynamic or the Maharishi's TM – while others are into weekend retreats with Zen masters, Hindu swamis, Tibetan lamas and new-age American teachers travelling the international guru trail. Without a doubt, meditation is moving into the mainstream.

Actually, what we're witnessing today is the groundswell of a revolution in social and personal consciousness that began some time ago. 'The rise in "inner-directed" people is manifesting in several different ways,' observed Peter Russell back in 1990 in a postscript to a new edition of *The Awakening Earth*. 'It can be seen in the increasing concern with physical fitness, organic food, not smoking and other changes which contribute to a person's health and well-being. It can be seen in the growing support for aid organizations and environmental groups, as people feel impelled by their own sense of right and wrong. It can be seen in the increasing number of people who question currently expected values and experiment with different, and perhaps more fulfilling, ways of living. And it can be seen in those who are seeking greater inner fulfilment through some spiritual discipline or in other ways of raising consciousness.'

And if Peter Mandel is right, this groundswell is about to become a torrent, a society-transforming tidal wave.

'It's becoming increasingly obvious that meditation is the path humanity as a whole is going to walk one day,' he said. 'That's why, more and more, I include meditation techniques in my seminars.' The aim is to equip the doctors, naturopaths and Colourpuncturists who attend his seminars with simple, effective methods for meditation which they can pass on to their patients.

'My effort was to find techniques that work instantaneously – for everyone, regardless of his or her level of consciousness,' he explained. 'I wanted to develop methods that create an immediate "Aha!" effect, that make people feel the life-force flowing through them. They may not understand the feeling, but if they experience it again and again, the longing for the light – which all humanity has – enters their lives. Certain structures become cleansed, and then, on their own, people set out on the path towards wholeness.'

One of his techniques uses the Esogetic Model, with its seven molecules transposed into circles of colour on a flag-like field of white cloth. He instructs people to stand on the molecules in a certain sequence, according to the points of the compass. In each direction, he said, something individual and different can be felt.

I tried it once, at a seminar in a conference hotel near the German spa of Bad Hersfeld. I no longer recall in which molecules I'd placed my feet nor the direction I was facing, but I fell suddenly silent and the most exquisite perfume filled the air. It was an instant whiff of another dimension, just as Mandel said there'd be.

His second group of what he calls 'unconscious meditations' involve the rose-quartz ball and a series of five archetypal postures inspired by images of ancient Egypt. We watched him demonstrate this technique at an international seminar on the Greek island of Corfu. Perched cross-legged on a table, slightly elevated above his audience, he assumed five positions, one after another – asking everyone, on each occasion, to focus on the ball in his hand for a few moments, and then, with eyes closed, to envision the ball dropping into their hearts.

Each posture moved me into a space of inner silence, but there was one in particular that, for me, made obvious his intent. The second I closed my eyes and, in my imagination, took the ball into my heart, I suddenly saw an Egyptian-style scarab, in brilliant colour, projected on to my inner screen. And it mirrored Mandel's posture precisely. All I recall about the rest of the day was a sense of freshness, a feeling of renewal, as if I'd just been to the ocean for an invigorating swim. To the early Egyptians, I discovered later, the scarab was revered as a symbol of resurrection. 'Aha!' I remember thinking, 'reborn' was exactly how I felt!

'In many cultures there are certain figures which create particular responses,' Mandel told us months afterwards in Bruchsal. 'This used to happen to me when I visited the Egyptian section at the Louvre in Paris, or read books about the ancient Celts. I would observe that something moved in me whenever I contemplated certain figures. And the experience somehow resonated in me, as if it were already known.

'Then, when I came across the rose-quartz ball, I intuitively knew that the vibration of the rose quartz was connected with the energy of the human heart, with love, with silence, with humility. And I suddenly had an urge to link these two things together.

'In that very moment, the five postures I use in the rose-quartz meditations came to me suddenly, as if someone had whispered what to do and how to do it into my ear. And I am a man who always trusts his "whisperings".

'Then I realized that if people take a rose-quartz ball home with them, and do these postures with their husbands or wives or their friends, they will embark on a journey towards their own inner guide. And it is the inner guide who switches on the light of consciousness, not the intellect.

'The great advantage of this kind of meditation is that people come to know their heart – without the interference of the intellect – since the frequency of the rose quartz is the frequency of the heart itself. That's why I tell people, in their imagination, to let the rose quartz roll into the heart, because this is where the energy of the rose quartz works. The heart is cleansed and strengthened, and people sense immediately that something special has taken place.

'My meditation techniques are not about effort or years of preparation, they are about experiencing and developing one's inner world in a very short space of time.'

Preparing for death and dying

Just as Mandel is working to bring meditation out of the spiritual closet – and demonstrate its effectiveness as a complementary tool for holistic healing – he is doing the same for dying, one of society's (and medicine's) greatest taboos.

'The majority of doctors can't deal with death and dying,' I was told by Dr Shobha Arturi, a graduate of the University of Milan, currently practising medicine, and Colourpuncture, in a small Tuscan town near Siena. And the failing of orthodox medicine, which turned her to Colourpuncture, was the lack of basic humanity with which many doctors behave.

'In medical school we were trained not to expose our personal feelings with patients, but to diagnose and treat with detachment, as if we were infallible,' she said. 'For me this was unbelievable! The truth is, doctors work in total insecurity. Treating the sicknesses of other human beings is such a great responsibility, one cannot help but be shaky. But to show this feeling is not allowed. Especially when faced with a patient who is dying. And death is going to happen to all of us one day, doctors included.'

The primary intent of Mandel's seminar on death and dying is to equip therapists and health practitioners with practical tools to support the dying process. The starting point is to relieve people's pain, and the next is to help them alleviate their fear.

'Fear of death is a basic tenet of Western religion,' he observed. 'We are taught that if we stray from God's laws we will suffer in hell when we die. This is a great tragedy. People who have grown up with a fear of death cannot understand the beauty of it.

'Ancient cultures saw death as part of life and taught their children how to die. When a family member died, the children were present so that they could observe the clarity and serenity of the transition to the next dimension.'

An anecdote from the life of Sarah Bernhardt illustrates his point. When Bernhardt's childhood nurse and lifelong companion lay dying, the French actress sat beside her bed. In the moment of death, she reported, the old woman's face shone with such light and bliss that Bernhardt knew, without a doubt, that death was an adventure to be welcomed, not a catastrophe to be feared.

But most people, it seems, die in panic, mentally and emotionally overwhelmed by a fear they are unequipped to master. And we cannot imagine the acute distress of someone who is flooded with pain. With pain or panic, there is no room for relaxation, no space for contemplating the transition that is coming.

Mandel's formula is, first of all, to alleviate the pain as much as possible – and second, to create an atmosphere of love, the polar opposite of fear.

'Every dying person needs a milieu of unconditional love, of intimacy and attention that asks for nothing in return,' he stated. The tool he teaches is touch – where to touch the dying person, precisely how to touch, and for what duration.

'Dying people need to feel that they are not alone, and touch is one of the most meaningful ways we human beings have of communicating love. Touch is a natural bioresonance, an invisible flow of love energy between people – and this is particularly important when someone is dying. The power of love is the greatest antidote to fear.'

The second component of his seminar on dying is Colourpuncture systems to help people deal with any unresolved conflicts that stand in the way of letting go – so that they can travel, as freely and unburdened as possible, on to the next dimension.

The focus of several of these systems is the unblocking, cleansing and energizing of the dying person's heart.

This is because, according to Mandel, existence moves us directly into the heart function circle at the moment of death – and since this function circle is also the seat of memory, dying becomes an opportunity to remember our unresolved conflicts, to resolve them at last, and then let them go.

Anyone who has gone through a near-death experience has witnessed this process, this replay of the memories stored in the heart. Faced with death, we find ourselves screening, on fast forward, the movie that has been our life – all the hurts we've suffered or inflicted, all the unfinished business, all the hopes and dreams still unfulfilled.

Mandel's approach supports this process of unburdening. He has developed systems – based on the four Tibetan bardos[1] of life, dying, after-death and rebirth – to provide an impulse for the realization that death is totally normal, that now it is time to go, that this life program is finished and that a new one awaits on the other side of death's door.

'All of these therapies are designed to help people get rid of the excess baggage of the life they are leaving during their last years, weeks or days,' he said. 'And this not only means setting their affairs in order and completing unfinished business, it also means cleaning up, as much as possible, whatever karma they have accumulated in this life.'

Karma is an Eastern concept – literally, the word means 'action' – and whether we Westerners acknowledge it or not, it plays a role in our living and dying as well. Karma is the law of cause and effect made manifest in man. It is recognizing that each of our actions triggers a result; it is reaping what we sow. As Padmasambhava, the father of Tibetan Buddhism, phrased it: 'If you want to know your past life, look into your present condition; if you want to know your past life, look into your present actions.' Karma is the stuff of learning; it is what taking total responsibility is all about.

'Karma is also the driving force behind reincarnation,' stated Mandel. 'And if a man can greet death in composure and without fear, at peace in the knowledge that he has completed, to the best of his ability, the karmas his actions have set in motion, he will be able to die consciously and carry with him, into the next incarnation, the benefit of the lessons he has learned in this life.'

'Although how or where we will be reborn is generally dependent on karmic forces, our state of mind at the time of death can influence the quality of our next rebirth,' wrote the Dalai Lama in his introduction to Sogyal Rinpoche's spiritual classic, *The Tibetan Book of Living and Dying*. 'So at the moment of death, in spite of the great variety of karmas we have accumulated, if we make a special effort to generate a virtuous state of mind, we may strengthen and activate a virtuous karma, and so bring about a happy rebirth.'

Full steam ahead

Peter Mandel's present incarnation began in a climate of pain and confusion, but now, in his mid-50s, he's reaping at last the fruits of his efforts and living a rich and rewarding life. His children from his first marriage have grown and prospered: Hans-Jürgen is a political economist and businessman, Alexander is pursuing a career in chemistry, and his daughter Martina is a naturopath at the Bruchsal practice. Mandel is happily remarried, with a new infant son – and after years of rebuffs from the scientific establishment, Esogetic medicine is proving its mettle and, in a growing number of countries, beginning to come into its own.

But Mandel's not a man to rest on any hard-won laurels; in terms of developing new systems, it's still full steam ahead. His first two children, Martina Schupeta and Markus Wunderlich – and one of Munich's best-known naturopaths, Robert Füss – are now sharing the load of workshops and seminars, as well as implementing a program of accreditation for Colourpuncture practitioners all over the world. And this is giving Mandel more freedom to do what it is he does best – listen to his whisperings, transform them into healing systems, and put them to work for the betterment of his fellow man.

And what's he working on at present? A myriad of things. He's building cosmic cones and DNA-like spirals to help him fathom the nature of energy and the mystery of time. He's continuing his exploration of the Kabbalah, establishing his own Esogetic numerology, discovering new relationships between man's implicit and explicit worlds – and finding, to give just one example, that the numbers of our birth name contain important clues to treating disorders of the spine. He's also taking the Transmitter Relays to higher levels, and uncovering new and unknown relationships between the individual and his uniquely personal pains.

His ongoing fascination with the workings of the brain and the origins of pain continues, and he's developing new, holographic interference and rose-quartz therapies, as well as a series of new colours for treatment, pre-spectral shades of the primordial grey. In addition, he's working with Dr Popp on the final stages of a special chamber in which a person's condition can be clearly diagnosed through biophoton emissions from the whole body, and not, as in his EEA system, only from fingers and toes. And, as to be expected, there is much, much more. At his home in Wiesloch are 15,000 sheets of A4 paper, covered with drawings and jottings for systems in development, and there are over 150 already completed but as yet unpublished, because, as he put it, 'It's not quite yet time'.

And what's the secret to all this creativity, to this endless outpouring of tried-and-tested treatments for harmonizing our physical ailments, for healing our psychological wounds? The answer, I am convinced, lies in surrender: in his conscious surrender to existence, to his individual life program; in stepping out of the way and letting the life-force flow through.

This is what began in Peter Mandel during those first days in Bruchsal, when he realized that existence had more in store for him than reading, that there must have been a purpose in life's rescuing him from death's door. Faced with the irrefutable, he surrendered: he put his trust and his future into life's hands. 'And from that moment,' he said (as the reader may remember), 'ideas and intuitions and systems broke over my head like an avalanche.'

Twenty years later, that avalanche is still rolling on. And shows no signs of abating. As Australian Colourpuncturist John Barlow remarked, 'Every time I start working with Peter Mandel's latest system, and think, "Now that's it; now he's finally covered every conceivable aspect of treating sickness and pain," he comes up with something totally new, some angle or approach that boggles my mind.'

I believe it's time for our minds to be boggled, not only John's, but yours and mine. We've been rooted in the past for so long we're running on empty. The planet is reeling from the weight of our waste, its ecobalance threatened by the greenhouse effect. And so much of life is unnatural, either saturated with chemicals or created from synthetics – the food we eat, the clothes we wear, the medicines we're prescribed to cure our ills. We've lost touch with nature, with the existential harmony; the part called man seems hell-bent on severing itself from the whole.

Then what can we do, you and I? We can begin by transforming ourselves, now, from precisely where we stand. We can start to free ourselves of imprints, of unresolved conflicts, and set out on the adventure to the source, to the truth of who we really are. We are microcosms of existence; existence is a macrocosm of us. And if we transform ourselves, the ripples of change reach others automatically – whether it's a small circle of family and friends and fellow workers, or, as in Mandel's case, doctors and naturopaths and people in pain all over the world.

Existence, I trust, is always ready to support our efforts to grow, to transform. The moment is ripe: we're on the threshold of a new millennium. And periods of transition are openings, crossroads, propitious opportunities for dropping the old and embarking upon the new.

We're moving from the Age of Pisces to the Age of Aquarius, where the earth will hang out for the next 2,000 years. And we only have to look back over the past two millennia to see that there's not much worth salvaging. The Piscean Age was a period of structured dependency and organized religion, of emotional slavery and the conflict of war. The Age of Aquarius, say astrologers, heralds a new possibility: the potential for acceptance and understanding, and the freedom that comes from being complete in oneself. It will be a time, we're told, of the maturing of spirit, of moving into, and functioning out of a higher frequency of the heart. Astrologers also call it the Cosmic Party, this Age of Light. And it goes into full swing, they tell us, on 21 December, the winter solstice of 2012. It's just around the corner. Now is the moment to prepare.

My experience of life tells me that there are no accidents, that whatever is needed is available at precisely the right time. And Peter Mandel is here and now, with a medicine of light for we beings of light. What could be more appropriate, I ask, for readying our emotional and physical bodies, and our spirits, for the transition to the dawning age?

Each morning, before my day begins, I sit outside on the terrace with a cup of tea. I listen to the songs of the birds; I watch the trees and the flowers saluting the sun. Inside and outside there is harmony: mine mirrored in existence; existence's reflected in mine. And Colourpuncture has had a lot to do with it. By cleansing and balancing our physical structures and emotional processes, it helps us realign ourselves with the innate harmony that is existence – and that is also the essential, unpolluted you and me.

Whether the Age of Light fulfils its promise is, for me, not really the point. My own age of light is manifesting already. And if there's ancillary support from the universe – a milieu of acceptance and understanding, of freedom and light – I'll welcome it with an open heart, with arms widespread. If there's a cosmic party coming, I have no intention of missing it. And neither, I hope, will you.

Notes

1 A light in the darkness

1 Source: *Esogetics: The Sense and Nonsense of Sickness and Pain*, by Peter Mandel and *Biophoton Emission: Experimental Background and Theoretical Approaches* by Fritz-Albert Popp, Qiau Gu and Ke-Hsueh Li, Modern Physics Letters B, vol. 8, nos 21 and 22 (1994), World Scientific Publishing Company.

2 The chakras are an integral component of Hindu yogic tradition. Named after the Sanskrit word for 'wheel', the chakras are invisible to the naked eye, yet are said, by mystics, to resemble whirling vortices of energy. There are seven chakras in all and their role, we are told, is to take in higher, cosmic energies and translate them into a form we are able to use to support physical and perceptual processes.

The seven chakras are said to be located on a vertical line running along the spine, from the coccyx to the top of the head.

The first, the root chakra, is situated at the base of the spine. It is associated with grounding, survival, vitality and male sexuality, and its related colour is red.

The second, the sacral chakra, is located in the lower belly just below the navel. It is associated with creativity, pleasure, desire, female sexuality, and is related to the colour orange.

The third, the solar plexus chakra, is located below the tip of the sternum. It is associated with the will and with personal power, and its related colour is yellow.

The fourth, the heart chakra, is in the centre of the chest. It is associated with unconditional love, forgiveness, compassion, consciousness, peace and tolerance. Its colour is green.

The fifth, the throat chakra, is associated with communication, expression and eloquence. Its colour is sky blue.

The sixth, known as the brow or 'third-eye' chakra, sits between the eyebrows. It is associated with intuition, imagination, concentration and visualization, and its related colour is indigo blue.

The final chakra, the crown chakra, is located on the top of the head. It is associated with wisdom, spirituality and cosmic consciousness. Its colour is violet.

3 DNA (deoxyribonucleic acid) is a complex giant molecule that contains, in chemically coded form, all the information needed to build, control and maintain a living organism. It is the DNA, unique in each of us, that sets us apart as individuals.

4 Georges Ivanovitch Gurdjieff (1866–1949) was a Russian-born mystic who, during the early part of the 20th century, travelled to Asia, Tibet and Egypt in search of spiritual enlightenment. He came across secret and esoteric schools; in particular, one ancient oral tradition he called the Work (also subsequently known as the Fourth Way) and brought back to the West – settling first in Russia and, after the revolution of 1917, near Paris. He wrote a number of books, including *Meetings with Remarkable Men*, an account of 'remarkable men' who had influenced his life. This explains my reference to 'Gurdjieffian' in relation to my first meeting with Peter Mandel.

Meetings with Remarkable Men was published after Gurdjieff's death. It was also made into a film by director Peter Brook in 1979 and starred Terence Stamp as G I Gurdjieff.

5 Emmanuel and Seth are popular 'channelled' entities.

Emmanuel is described as a 'being of golden light' by the American channel Pat Rodegast, through whom 'he' has been communicating for some 15 years. Transcripts of sessions with Emmanuel are published in *Emmanuel's Book* and *Emmanuel's Book II: The Choice for Love*.

Seth is probably the best-known of these channelled entities, and was one of the first to achieve prominence. He spoke through an American woman called Jane Roberts, who died in 1984. The transcripts of her more than 1,800 sessions with Seth over 20-odd years fill nine published books.

2 Beings of light

1 The functions of the subtle bodies of light that comprise the human energy field, or aura, are detailed in chapter 4, 'Energy Speaks'.

To embrace the notion that the seat of emotion lies in one of our energy bodies requires an holistic view of the human being. We are the sum total of seven bodies, of which only one, the physical body, is visible to the naked eye. Historically, the ability to see the aura in its entirety has been the province of psychics and clairvoyants. In the 20th century, however, technology has been developed which has proven that luminescent energy fields surround all living organisms.

Down the ages, the view was held that the physical body occupied the central position in our being, and that the subtle bodies that comprise the aura emanated outward from the physical. Today, that belief has been replaced by the understanding that all seven bodies are interconnected and interdependent, and that, energetically, the physical body is actually the most dense – and that higher energies are 'stepped down' through the various bodies before manifesting on the physical plane. This is supported by the work of clairvoyants like American physicist-turned-healer Barbara Ann Brennan who can 'see', in the aura, organ malfunctions which, if left untreated, will eventually manifest in the physical body as a sick organ.

In a similar fashion, emotions originate in the astral or emotional energy body and manifest in this dimension. There are those who also say that 'the mind' is also housed in one of these subtle energy bodies and not, as science has speculated for years, buried somewhere in the recesses of the brain.

2 Zen is short for Zen Buddhism. It has its roots in the patriarch Bodhidharma who took the teachings of Gautam Buddha from India to China around AD 475. In China, Buddhism mingled with Taoism and the 'Ch'an' school of Buddhism was the result. From China, 'Ch'an' travelled to Japan around AD 1200, and became known as Zen.

Zen is more of an individual approach to spiritual awakening than a philosophy or a religious approach. One of its central points is intuitive understanding – with logic viewed as irrelevant and words seen as having no fixed meaning. What is important is who is speaking, who is being spoken to, and the situation in which the words are used. In Japan, a whole range of activities have been strongly influenced by Zen, from drawing and calligraphy and anecdotes, to tea drinking, music and martial arts. In Zen, the meaning is invariably to be found between the lines.

3 The body's circadian rhythm is its metabolic rhythm, and generally coincides with our 24-hour day. The most apparent manifestation of our circadian rhythm is the cycle of sleeping and waking.

4 A photomultiplier is an instrument for detecting low levels of light and amplifying the light to produce a detectable and measurable signal up to 100 million times larger than the original signal. Similar devices, called image intensifiers, are used in television camera tubes that 'see' in the dark.

5 The concept of the Akashic records is an ancient one, found in the early esoteric literature of many cultures. In *Vibrational Medicine*, author Dr Richard Gerber compares the Akashic records to a 'universal candid camera' in which everything that happens, has happened and will happen, is recorded. Accessibility to the data contained in the

Akashic records apparently depends on a highly and finely developed consciousness.

6 Source: *About the Nature of Biophotons* by W P Mei, from *Journal of Biological Systems*, vol. 2, no. 1 (1994) 25–42, World Scientific Publishing Company.

There are similarities with the capacity we call 'memory'. The human memory automatically 'records' events as they transpire, and retains that record in some kind of accessible data bank. How memory actually functions, though, remains one of the great unsolved mysteries.

Rupert Sheldrake (author of *The Rebirth of Nature* and other books) is a biologist who views creation as a living organism, rather than 'a machine with God as the great mechanic'. Sheldrake is perhaps best known for his hypothesis of morphic resonance and morphic fields. Fundamentally, he says that the development of all organisms, from a baby in the womb to a tree from a seed, depends on organizing fields he calls morphic (from the Greek for 'form'). He says that the organization of behaviour – such as the instincts that govern the behaviour of an ant, for example – also depend on morphic fields. In relation to our mental life, he sets forth a similar hypothesis.

Sheldrake sees these morphic fields as the organizing fields of nature, and believes that much of what we and other organisms inherit depends on the cumulative memory of the species that is carried within these fields. Although these fields are largely determined by habit, Sheldrake points out that they are not static, because existence is always open to the new. In an interview published on the Internet, he cites the following example: 'At some stage somebody invented the bicycle. For the first time, the bicycle was made. For the first time somebody rode a bicycle. Before that, there hadn't been a habit of bicycle riding; and I think precisely because so many people have that habit, it is easier for everybody else to learn to ride bicycles, on average, by morphic resonance from this habitual activity. In other words, there are now morphic fields for bicycle making and bicycle riding, and it must embrace the whole planet in a way that didn't exist at one time.'

4 Energy speaks

1 In a contributing section to Mandel's book, *Lichtblicke in der ganzheitlichen (Zahn-) Medizin* (Ray of Light in Holistic Dentistry), published by Energetik-Verlag in 1989 (but unpublished to date in English) biophysicist Dr Fritz-Albert Popp offers a layman's explanation of what transpires in the process of Kirlian photography.

He begins by tracing the roots of the Kirlian technique to the experiments of Georg Christian Lichtenberg, the 17th-century German physicist who proved that, in fields of high electric charges, a discharge of gas was produced as soon as the bursting point of the gas was exceeded. These phenomena were accompanied by light emissions which came to be known as Lichtenberg emissions.

'Today we know all about gas discharge,' Popp wrote. 'Each and every light tube is based on this principle. All the more surprising, then, that only very few people seem to know that Kirlian photography is making use of the same qualities of high sensitivity that were typical of the Lichtenberg emissions; this hypersensitivity enables the most subtle of differences in the static and dynamic electric charges of the human skin to become visible . . .

'Kirlian photography can differentiate even the most minute charges on the human skin and render them clearly visible down to one hundredth of a millimetre. In simple terms, this is what happens: within fractions of a second the skin surface, placed against an anti-electrode, is given a charge high enough for it to release, via field emission, electric charges with a kinetic energy of some kilo-electron volts, high enough to ionize the surrounding gas a thousand times. The gas thus stimulated releases a "recombination light" which is captured photographically.

'Basically what happens is similar to a very common experience: crossing a carpet of synthetic material, we accumulate an electric charge, and when we touch a doorknob, sparks fly. Kirlian photography is nothing but the trick of capturing this very process so that it can be reproduced with utmost exactness, and in such a way that no harm or pain is incurred during the discharge.'

2 The rate of circulation of the *ch'i* through the body's invisible network of meridians was established by two French doctors, Jean-Claude Darras and Pierre de Vernejoul in 1986. According to a report in *Electromagnetic Man* by Cyril Smith and Simon Best (J M Dent & Sons Ltd, London 1989), Darras and de Vernejoul injected a radioactive tracer solution at an acupuncture point and ascertained, through the use of a gamma-ray camera, that the radioactivity travelled along the acupuncture meridian at a speed of between three and five centimetres per minute. This translates, by their calculations, into 25 circulations per day or night.

3 Voll's technique is known as EAV, for Electroacupuncture According to Voll. As well as discovering new meridians, Voll developed a widely used device called the Voll Machine for either measuring the electrical level of acupuncture points (and associated organ functions) or for treating acupuncture points by the administration of an electrical charge.

5 The holistic miracle

1 Sebastian Kneipp (1821–97) was a German Catholic priest, renowned for his generosity of heart and his charitable works, particularly with the ill and downtrodden. He developed a system known as Kneipp Therapy, wrote three books on healing and prevention, and built three sanatoria where patients were treated with his combination of water therapy, herbs, diet and exercise. Today, his therapies are used at many spas and institutes in Europe, and his techniques are taught in physiotherapy schools in Germany, Switzerland and other countries.

Samuel Hahnemann (1755–1842), a German physician, developed homoeopathy, an holistic medical system widely practised today in many countries around the world. Based on the writings of Hippocrates in the 5th century, the experiments of Paracelsus in the 16th, and Hahnemann's own observations, homoeopathy treats sickness via the principle of 'similars' – *similia similibus curentur*, let like be cured with like. Its remedies consist of infinitesimal doses of whatever malady affects the patient, in much the same way as inoculation with minute cultures of chickenpox or diphtheria immunizes children against these diseases.

Allopathy, a term coined by Hahnemann from the Greek for 'opposite suffering', followed the antithetical route, treating with 'contraries'. For example, an allopathic doctor will prescribe a laxative for constipation. This relieves the constipation, but can trigger the opposite condition, diarrhoea. Allopathy isn't so concerned with *why* the patient might be constipated, with what it is about his lifestyle or his emotional state that is binding his bowels; it is more into alleviating the symptom than concerning itself with the underlying cause.

To all but American readers, homoeopathy is probably familiar. It came to America in the 1820s, at a time when archaic treatments like bloodletting were all the vogue, and large numbers of homoeopathic hospitals, sanatoria and training colleges soon sprang up across the country. But over the next 50 years the allopathic brotherhood managed to eradicate it. This was the time of the introduction of penicillin, the new cure-all, and the American Medical Association, with the help of the pharmaceutical industry, mounted a huge anti-homoeopathy propaganda campaign and closed many homoeopathic teaching institutions. By 1918, homoeopathy's brief American heyday was over.

In the past 15 years there has been a resurgence of interest in homoeopathy in the USA, with an estimated 3,000 physicians and other health-care practitioners using homoeopathy, according to a 1990 survey. This same report indicated, however, that only one per cent of the general population, or 2.5 million people, visited a homoeopathic doctor that year. (Source: *Alternative Medicine: Expanding Medical Horizons*, published in 1992 by the Office of Alternative Medicine, National Institutes of Health, USA.)

2 The Pharos at Alexandria was the first known lighthouse and one of the seven wonders of the ancient world.

3 Alchemy is the art of transformation. During the Middle Ages, it was understood as the search for 'the philosopher's stone' by which base metals such as lead could be transformed into gold. The philosopher's stone was also thought to hold the secret to eternal life. Today, we understand alchemy as the quest for a means by which man (base metal) can become one with the spirit (gold) that is his true nature. Owing to the repressive nature of the Christian Church of the period, and its penchant for burning so-called heretics, it is also thought that the alchemists of the day protected themselves by hiding the spiritual nature of their work and presenting themselves as 'chemists' involved in mundane experimentation.

4 For readers unfamiliar with French sweets, my dictionary describes a *madeleine* as a small sponge cake, often coated with jam and coconut.

5 This reflex zone is located at the top of the neck, at the junction of the cervical vertebrae and the skull. Here, there is a protruding bone; the reflex zone is found in the indentation immediately under this bone.

6 Holographic healing

1 GV 20 is the standard abbreviation for acupuncture point number 20 on the Governing Vessel (GV) meridian. This meridian begins in the pelvic cavity and, ascending along the spinal column, continues over the top of the head and down across the forehead and nose to end inside the upper gum. (There are also internal branches of this meridian reaching the kidneys and into the brain.)

Each of the body's meridians is identified by a specific name – Governing Vessel, Conception Vessel, Liver Meridian, Pericardium Meridian, Kidney Meridian, etc. – and each is given an appropriate abbreviation to guide practitioners. For locating specific acupuncture points along each meridian, points are also numbered; eg, GV 20.

7 A new paradigm for prevention

1 Other examples of interference: interference of white (or multi-wavelength) light results in coloured fringes of the spectral colours, such as

the iridescent colours a film of oil produces on water. In the case of monochromatic (or single wavelength) light, interference produces patterns of light or dark bands. Interference of sound waves of similar frequency results in 'beats'.

9 A tool for consciousness

1 *Bardo* is a Tibetan word for the gap that occurs between the completion of one situation and the commencement of another. Tibetan philosophy speaks of four bardos: the 'natural' bardo of living, the 'painful' bardo of dying, the 'luminous' bardo of the after-death experience, and the 'karmic' bardo of becoming, of the period leading up to rebirth. According to Tibetan tradition, each bardo contains possibilities for awakening, for liberation from the cycle of life and death.

Bibliography

Alder, Vera Stanley. *The Secret of the Atomic Age*, Rider Books, 1988.

Chopra, Deepak MD. *Quantum Healing*, Bantam Books, 1990.

Foster, David. *The Intelligent Universe*, Abelard-Schumann, 1975.

Gerber, Richard, MD. *Vibrational Medicine*, Bear & Co. 1988.

Hay, Louise L. *Heal Your Body*, Specialist Publications, 1989.

Liberman, Jacob, OD, Ph.D. *Light: Medicine of the Future*, Bear & Co., 1991.

Mandel, Peter. *Practical Compendium of Colourpuncture, Volume 1*, Energetik-Verlag, 1986.

Mandel, Peter. *Acupunct-Impulser-Therapy*, Energetik-Verlag, 1988.

Mandel, Peter. *Energy Emission Analysis*, Energetik-Verlag, 1991.

Mandel, Peter. *Esogetics: The Sense and Nonsense of Sickness and Pain*, Energetik-Verlag, 1993.

Mandel, Peter and Pflegler, Andreas. *Colors: The Pharmacy of Light*, Energetik-Verlag, 1997.

Popp, Dr Fritz-Albert. *Biologie des Lichts*, Paul Parey, 1984.

Popp, Dr Fritz-Albert. *Die Botschaft der Nahrung*, Fischer Taschenbuch Verlag, 1993.

Rinpoche, Sogyal. *The Tibetan Book of Living and Dying*, Rider Books, 1992.

Russell, Peter. *The Awakening Earth*, Arkana, 1991.

Sacks, Oliver. *The Man Who Mistook His Wife for a Hat*, Picador, 1986.

Siegel, Bernie S. MD. *Love, Medicine and Miracles*, Arrow Books, 1988.

Talbot, Michael. *The Holographic Universe*, Grafton Books, 1991.

Tibbs, Hardwin. *The Future of Light*, Watkins Publishing, 1981.

Useful addresses

For information about Esogetic Medicine and Colourpuncture practitioners and seminars in Europe, Australia and other English-speaking countries, please contact the following organizations:

International Mandel Institute for Esogetic Medicine
Wesemlinstrasse 2
CH-6000 Lucerne 6
Switzerland
Tel: +41-(0)41-4 20 60 24
Fax: +41-(0)41-4 20 60 25

Mandel Institute
Hildastrasse 8
D-76646 Bruchsal
Germany
Tel: +49-(0)7251-80 01 40
Fax: +49-(0)7251-80 01 55

For information about Esogetic Medicine and Colourpuncture practitioners and seminars in North America, please contact:

Akhila Dass, O.M.D., L.Ac.
Institute for Esogetic Colorpuncture and Kirlian Photography
P.O. Box 3013
San Anselmo, CA 94979
USA
Tel: (415) 461-6641
Fax: (415) 461 0831

Manohar Croke, BA
Institute for Esogetic Colorpuncture and Kirlian Photography
1705 14th Street, #198
Boulder, CO 80302
USA
Tel: (303) 443-1666/938-9189
Fax: (303) 516-0059

For information about Colourpuncture sets, Kirlian machines, Esogetic products and books by Peter Mandel, please contact:

Kamla GmbH or Energetik Verlag GmbH
Hildastrasse 8
D-76646 Bruchsal
Germany
Tel: +49-(0)7251-80 01 35
Fax: +49-(0)7251-80 01 55

For detailed information on the Migraine and Childhood Insomnia studies outlined in chapter 6, contact:

Dr Fausto Pagnamenta
Via Ospedale 14
CH-6600 Locarno
Switzerland
Tel: +41-(0)91-751 16 24
Fax: +41-(0)91-751 55 61

Index

Hypothalamus ~~controls~~ thorn? pit. gland

controls a wide range of bodily ~~symptoms~~ functions which are influenced by light. The hyp. is energized by external light. → pit → hormone

Hormonal system: — pituitary, pineal, thyroid, thymus, adrenals, pancreas + gonads.

Pineal gland = 3rd eye

Ht / si

connected to blood circulatory system + wisdom teeth.
Sensory organ: TONGUE. (speech).

Sp. St - (MALE)

Basic function: thinking
Sp. St, pancreas, throat, joints, 2 molar teeth.
Sensory organ: MOUTH + LIPS
touching tasting chewing swallowing (meditate!)

Lu, LI -

Basic function: intuiting
Lu, LI, premolars (teeth 4+5), skin, hair, immune system.
external organ = NOSE
Holding on, resisting change, unworthy, acute grief, heartache.

Liv, Gb →

Basic function: feeling
emotional: anger/rage.
Li, gb, muscles, sinews, canine teeth.
Sensory organ = EYE

ki / bl: - kidneys, bladder, lymph, genitals,
ovaries, bones, knees, 4 front up + lower teeth
Basic function: sensing
emotional: fear.
Difficulty accepting unawareness, or listen to intuition
Sensory organ = EAR

(132)

FEMALE - ki, bl + lu, li,
MALE - Li, gb + sp. st.
ELBOWS: from liver/gall: anger - need flex + tolerance

Printed in the United Kingdom
by Lightning Source UK Ltd.
93495

9 781843 331247